STRATEGY ANALYSIS WITH
ValueWar

Mark J. Chussil
David J. Reibstein

▲ *The Scientific Press*

Strategy Analysis with ValueWar
by Mark J. Chussil and David J. Reibstein

Acquisitions Editor: Peter W. Fairchild
Production Editor and Text Design: Mark J. Chussil
Cover Design: Rogondino & Associates

© 1994 by Advanced Competitive Strategies, Inc.

 boyd & fraser publishing company
A Divison of South-Western Publishing Co.
One Corporate Place • Ferncroft Village
Danvers, Massachusetts 01923

 The Scientific Press is a division of boyd & fraser publishing company.

 International Thomson Publishing
boyd & fraser publishing company is an ITP company.
The ITP trademark is used under license.

Manufactured in the United States of America

ISBN 0-89426-241-6   (with 3.50″ disk)
ISBN 0-89426-242-4   (with 5.25″ disk)

10 9 8 7 6 5 4 3 2 1

 This book is printed on recycled, acid-free paper that meets Environmental Protection Agency standards.

Contents

ValueWar Reference   1

Strategy Analysis with ValueWar

ValueWar™ is state-of-the-art computer software that simulates the effects of your strategy and your competitors' strategies on your business's competitive and financial performance. You can use ValueWar to test the consequences of your decisions (and your competitors') the easy way — on your computer — before you invest years of effort and risk millions of dollars.

Managers find that the business principles in ValueWar simulations are familiar, intuitive, and easy to apply. These principles range from the obvious, such as the effects of market growth rates and price elasticities on customer demand, to the subtle, such as the propensity of large competitors to ignore the actions of small competitors. All told, ValueWar takes about seventy such factors into account in its simulations, producing the high degree of realism that managers need in a strategy-analysis tool.

The demonstration copy of ValueWar that accompanies this book is the full ValueWar software, minus only the software that you would use to "calibrate" ValueWar for your business. You'll see ValueWar in action with the demo and this book, but please remember that ValueWar's analysis with the demo calibration will bear little resemblance to the simulations it would produce after being calibrated for your business.

If this book accompanies the full ValueWar package, including the ValueWar Calibrator™ software, then you can use this book to get ideas for how to run ValueWar for your business situations. It also provides key information that you can use to calibrate scenarios.

Strategy Analysis with ValueWar will show you how ValueWar simulations offer new insights into principles of competitive strategy and into the strategic decisions that every business has to make.

Strategy Analysis with ValueWar describes ValueWar from three perspectives:

- *About ValueWar*
- The *ValueWar Tutorial*
- The *ValueWar Reference*.

About ValueWar

About ValueWar talks about why you'd want to use ValueWar in the first place. It shows how ValueWar offers you a unique and powerful tool for testing strategies *before* you commit time, money, and resources to them.

We strongly recommend that you read *About ValueWar* no matter which other sections of *Strategy Analysis with ValueWar* you plan to read.

ValueWar Tutorial

The *ValueWar Tutorial* gives you hands-on experience with the ValueWar software and analyses by running a simple case analysis through ValueWar. Use the *Tutorial* if you want to see what ValueWar does and why it does it.

Chapter 1, *Installing ValueWar*, tells you how to install the software.

Chapter 2, *Basic ValueWar*, concentrates on the basics of the software. It starts an analysis that Chapter 4 concludes and that Chapter 5 analyzes.

Chapter 3, *More ValueWar Features*, takes a brief detour from strategy analysis to cover ValueWar's power-user specialties: graphs, reports, "animation," and context-sensitive help. These features make ValueWar both more enjoyable and more insightful to use.

Chapter 4, *Advanced ValueWar*, describes more-advanced analytic features of ValueWar. It extends the analysis begun in Chapter 2, focusing on ValueWar's variety of "what-if" tests.

Chapter 5, *ValueWar In Depth*, walks page-by-page through the results of the simulation you ran in Chapters 2 and 4. It includes the full text of a ValueWar report.

Chapter 6, *Analyzing ValueWar*, appraises strategy implications from the *Tutorial's* analysis. It also introduces several kinds of advanced analysis. You can experiment with some of these analyses with the demonstration version of ValueWar.

If you want to understand strategy analysis with ValueWar, be sure to read *Tutorial* Chapter 6. If you're focusing on the results of ValueWar simulations, read Chapter 5. If you want to learn the capabilities of the software, concentrate on Chapters 2, 3, and 4.

The ValueWar Reference

The *Reference* section offers more technical detail about how ValueWar works. It will help answer questions about the factors and procedures ValueWar uses to simulate competition.

The *Reference* contains three sections:

1 Scenario Reference. Describes the factors that ValueWar uses to simulate competition and the market environment.

2 Strategy Reference. Describes how ValueWar strategies work.

3 Keyboard Reference. Provides a compact summary of the keys you can use with ValueWar and what they do.

About ValueWar's authors

Mark J. Chussil is co-founder and President of Advanced Competitive Strategies, Inc. He is also Visiting Lecturer at the Aresty Institute of Executive Education at the Wharton School of the University of Pennsylvania. Together with ACS co-founder David Reibstein, Mark developed ValueWar.

Mark works actively with ACS clients using ValueWar and other ACS services in a variety of industries. He also designs an ongoing series of enhancements to the ValueWar software. He speaks frequently at companies, conferences, and seminars about using competitive simulations to develop successful competitive strategies.

Previously, Mark spent 15 years at the Strategic Planning Institute (The PIMS Program), where he was Director, Business-Unit Strategy Research and Director, PC Products. At SPI he developed new methodologies and software for analyzing business strategies, performed and published basic research on the PIMS data base, taught business strategy at companies and universities, and wrote and managed the PIMS/PC™ software.

Mark's work experience also includes three years in strategic planning at Sequent Computer Systems in Beaverton, Oregon, a major producer of high-performance multiprocessing computers. He introduced and applied quantitative techniques to strategy problems such as making tradeoffs among corporate measures of success and installing a program to measure and monitor market-perceived quality.

Mark's articles and case studies on business strategy have appeared in the *Sloan Management Review*, *Planning Review*, *The Journal of Business Strategy*, *PC World*, and many other publications. He has spoken on quality and competitive strategy at numerous companies, universities, and conferences. Mark's professional interests focus on topics such as applying quantitative techniques to real-world business-strategy problems, the link between market-perceived quality and financial performance, and executive education.

Mark earned his M.B.A. in General Management from Harvard University and his B.A. in Political Science from Yale University.

David J. Reibstein is the William S. Woodside Professor and Professor of Marketing at the Wharton School of the University of Pennsylvania. From 1987 to 1992 he was the Julian Aresty Professor of Marketing and Vice Dean of the Wharton School, and Director of the Wharton/PIMS Research Center. He is also co-founder and Chairman of Advanced Competitive Strategies, Inc. Together with ACS co-founder Mark Chussil, he developed ValueWar.

Prior to his appointment at Wharton, he served for five years as Assistant Professor of Marketing at the Harvard Business School (1975-80). He was also a Visiting Professor of Marketing at INSEAD in Fontainebleau, France (1983) and at Stanford University (1987). At Wharton he teaches Marketing Management and Marketing Research in the MBA program. He developed and coordinated Wharton's Executive Seminar on New Product Development and Marketing Research, as well as several others. He was featured in *Fortune* magazine as one of the nation's eight "Favorite Business School Professors." He has received the Wharton School's Excellence in Teaching Award every year since it was initiated in 1982. In 1987 he won the honor at the Wharton School for having the best student ratings over the preceding two years. Prior to his academic career Professor Reibstein was employed in the marketing department of Sauter Laboratories, a division of Hoffman-LaRoche Pharmaceutical Company.

Professor Reibstein is the author of *Marketing: Concepts, Strategies, and Decisions* and co-author of *Cases in Marketing Research*, both published by Prentice-Hall, Inc. He also has authored numerous articles appearing in major marketing journals, including recent publications in the *Journal of Marketing Research*, *Marketing Science*, *Harvard Business Review*, *Journal of Advertising Research*, *Journal of Marketing*, and *Journal of Consumer Research*. His primary research interests are in market segmentation, marketing models, and understanding brand choice behavior. He has consulted and run executive programs for a number of companies including AT&T, General Electric, Digital Equipment Company, Rohm and Haas, Dean Witter Reynolds, Campbell's Soup, and numerous others.

Professor Reibstein received his Ph.D. in Industrial Administration at Purdue University, was in the MBA program at Tulane University, and obtained his B.A. in Statistics and Political Science and his B.S. in Business Administration at the University of Kansas. He also received an honorary Masters from the University of Pennsylvania.

Advanced Competitive Strategies is founded on the belief that winning strategies result from combining management creativity with state-of-the-art planning technology. ACS specializes in these technologies and methods:

- **ValueWar**: Interactive simulation of strategy alternatives.

- **MPQ**: Quantitative measurement of market-perceived quality.

- **Strategic Tradeoffs™**: Alignment of management values around a common definition of success.

ACS clients include Fortune-500 corporations in a variety of industries, small high-tech companies, and universities.

If you have any questions or comments about ValueWar or Advanced Competitive Strategies, please feel free to contact Mark or Dave. You can reach Mark at ACS headquarters in Portland, Oregon, (503) 243-2586. You can reach Dave at the Wharton School, (215) 898-6643.

Acknowledgments

I believe that ValueWar is part of the revolution in thinking and technology that is just starting to affect the way industry develops competitive strategies. This revolution combines what people do best — creating, imagining, dreaming — with the power of computers to simulate what those creative, imaginative, and visionary futures would look like.

A work of this scope, combining a book on advanced concepts in strategic thought with hundreds of pages worth of computer code, draws on the knowledge, insight, skills, goodwill, and partnership of many people.

My parents, Yale Chussil and Janet Fein, and my brother Paul taught me to value learning. Their gift gave me the curiosity and dedication to pursue the ideas in this book and software, and I hope that their pride in this accomplishment repays my debt to them in some small way.

My colleagues at Sequent Computer Systems invited me to share the computer industry roller coaster. I am particularly indebted to Dr. Gael Curry and Michael Simon for their deep insights into blending strategy and people, and for their tireless efforts to teach those insights to me.

Peter Fairchild, General Manager of the Scientific Press, has made the publication of this book an enjoyable experience. He has been an enthusiastic business partner and a real pleasure to do business with.

Many people have used ValueWar in industry and in education. There are far too many to thank here, but I want to mention Brian Johnston, Betty Noonan, and Joseph Paul at Eastman Kodak Company; the late Carrie Solin of Rohm & Haas Company; Jim Keller, David McAuliffe, Mary Redd, and Lou Vargha of Weyerhaeuser Paper Company; and the hundreds of participants at the *Competitive Marketing Strategy* seminar at the Aresty Institute of Executive Education at the Wharton School.

I found my 15 years at the Strategic Planning Institute (SPI, also known as The PIMS Program) to be a continuous source of education. Although it is inanimate (and incorporeal), I enjoyed tremendous enlightenment from working with the PIMS data base. Among my human benefactors at SPI, I thank Ruth Newman (no longer with SPI) for teaching me to work with words and Don Swire for teaching me to work with numbers.

Joaquim Branco, formerly of SPI and now a principal at Mantis Associates, is a rare computer virtuoso. He transferred as much of his wizardry (and humor) to me as my poorer talents were able to absorb, and became a dear friend in the process.

Mindy Clark and Joanne Kahn, both Vice Presidents of Advanced Competitive Strategies, have been instrumental in bringing ValueWar to industry. They were among the first to embrace ValueWar, and they have contributed their ideas, energy, and enthusiasm toward its continuous improvement. It is an honor and a delight to work with them.

When I mentioned before that I have learned from the PIMS data base, that means in large measure that I have learned from Dr. Sidney Schoeffler, Founding Director of the Strategic Planning Institute and currently principal of Mantis Associates. But Sid's role goes far, far beyond that. Sid was my mentor during and since our SPI days. He is a true visionary in the field of strategic planning, a brilliant thinker, a mesmerizing orator, and a gifted teacher. Sid has profoundly shaped my career and how I think, and I thank him deeply for his help and friendship.

I met Dave Reibstein in the late 1970s in his classroom at the Harvard Business School. I was immediately impressed with his awesome intellect, his personal warmth and his, ah, unusual (and devastatingly quick) sense of humor. Dave is simply the finest teacher I have ever seen, combining a grandmaster's knowledge of competitive strategy and a statistician's knowledge of quantitative techniques with a true gift for transfering that knowledge to his students and to ValueWar. ValueWar would not be what it is, and I would not be what I am (an opening for a Reibstein rapier if ever there was one!), without Dave. I thank him for his patience and teaching, and I thank him, his wife Karen, and his children Sasha and Seth, for making me feel part of their family. I am proud to call Dave my partner and dear friend.

My wife Janice has lived with the crushing hours, the curses at stubborn computers, the obsession and the elation of a new book and a new product. And while she has borne far more inconvenience than I had any right to ask, she has so much grace, strength, and love that she repaid me with endless support and encouragement. I simply could not have contributed as I have to this book and software without her. Janice, I can never repay what I owe you and I can never express how much you mean to me, but I'll never stop trying. Thank you for true love.

Mark J. Chussil
August 1993

When you write a book the greatest excitement is that it's done. Now back to life as a real person. It's then you realize that that life, as a real person, is no different, with backed-up work, other half-way completed projects, and new ventures yearning to be completed.

This book completion feels different. We have written the last page, and it's far from over. The excitement is not for its culmination, but for its marking of a beginning. Simulations have been around for a long time. Their use as a business tool for strategy development is in its embryonic stages, however.

So, there is no relief it is over, but excitement about the beginning. Nonetheless, it is a good time to momentarily pause to acknowledge those who helped get us to this stage. This would have to include colleagues, educators, collaborators, friends, and family.

A large number of educators may be accused of letting me slip through the system. Many of them even taught me something along the way. The one who deserves to be singled out is my dissertation advisor, Frank M. Bass. Not only did he teach me most of what I know about marketing analysis, he also taught me the importance not just of learning, but also of educating. He did it all through example and is one of the best educators I know. He is dedicated to finding answers.

I have a number of colleagues whose ideas have seemed to find their way into what I call my work. Clearly it belongs to them. Much of their contributions have been in terms of ideas, critical thinking, and as role models. My colleagues while I was on the faculty at the Harvard Business School were first to instill in me the need for practicality for real-world problems. My fellow faculty since I have been at The Wharton School for more than the past dozen years have stressed for me the need to be productive and the need to work on future problems, not reiterations of those in the past. In particular, Professor Jerry Wind, aside from being a great friend and a constant tennis nemesis, has taught me not to think in constraints or of projects with only minimal incremental impact, but rather that the only perspective to take is of big projects with the potential for significant impact. If I could only keep up with his 25 hours per day, 8 days per week schedule, I could learn to be even more productive.

My friends Professors David Weinstein of INSEAD and Paul Farris at the Darden School, have to be mentioned not only because of their constant collaboration with me throughout the years, but also because they may never speak to me again if I fail to mention them.

Additionally, special thanks must be given to my assistant, Ms. Heidi Brown. Not only does she tolerate my disorganization and unreasonable demands, she reinforces these behaviors by her high level of response and performance. She deserves more than mere thanks.

While all of the above individuals have contributed to my teachings, work ethic and occasionally lack thereof, and perspective of what should constitute accomplishment, this specific project would never have been attempted, completed, or taken to its next level without Mark Chussil. I first met Mark as a student of mine at Harvard Business School. What the world doesn't sufficiently understand, it is from the best of students that teachers often learn. Mark has been a standout. Mark and I may debate whose brainchild ValueWar is (which means it is probably Mark's). However, his designs and his attentiveness to details (all who know him know this part must be true) allowed ValueWar to move from just a concept to a truly alive and vivid simulation. He combines the skills of one of the best computer experts with an acute understanding of strategic concepts and their application.

Lastly, of course, I must give my sincerest thanks and love to my family. This begins with my parents, Joel and Bessie who taught me business, hard work, love and humor — all of which were necessary in this endeavor. My young older brother, Larry, has always served as my hardest critic (as any brother should), yet at the same time being extremely supportive.

The balance in my life comes from my lovely wife, Karen, and our two children (the Koozels) Sasha and Seth. Upon arriving home it becomes quite apparent (pun intended) what is truly important. Sasha and Seths' growth and development provides the same for their parents. Karen is the perfect mother and wife. Persevering with my life and frenetic pace/schedule deserves a medal. Instead, she will have to settle for my love.

David J. Reibstein
August 1993

Dedication

To my very lovable wife, Janice.
Thank you for choosing me.

Mark J. Chussil

To my lovely and loving parents,
Joel and Bessie Reibstein.

David J. Reibstein

ABOUT ValueWar

About ValueWar

ValueWar™ is state-of-the-art computer software that simulates the effects of your strategy and your competitors' strategies on your business's competitive and financial performance. You can use ValueWar to test the consequences of your decisions (and your competitors') the easy way — on your computer — before you invest years of effort and risk millions of dollars.

ValueWar simulations are tailored to your business. The factors that drive ValueWar simulations are set to values appropriate for your business in a process called "calibration." Calibration makes ValueWar work for your business and its unique competitive situation.

The calibration process itself helps you learn about your business. Managers find that ValueWar raises critical questions that traditional planning processes overlook. Some even use ValueWar as a way to organize their strategic information and to understand its implications.

As we have learned applying ValueWar in industry and in executive education, managers find that the business principles in ValueWar simulations are familiar, intuitive, and easy to apply. All told, ValueWar takes about seventy factors into account in its simulations, producing the realism that managers need in a strategy-analysis tool.

- Should you retaliate if your biggest competitor cuts prices 20%?
- How should you position your products and services?
- Should you hide your strategy from your competitors?
- Will zero defects help you gain market share?
- Should you base compensation on performance?
- Will your competitive strategy work?

ValueWar helps you test your decisions before you invest years of effort and risk millions of dollars

ValueWar simulations

The Pentagon plays "war games."

Athletes shadow-box, spar, scrimmage, and spring-train.

Actors rehearse.

Lawyers try mock cases.

Engineers test prototypes.

Pilots fly flight simulators.

Architects build scale models.

Physicians and scientists conduct experiments.

What do businesspeople do?

In practically every human endeavor in which decisions have far-reaching consequences, it is customary to simulate the possible outcomes of those decisions. Indeed, we consider it irresponsible *not* to perform those tests. Who would fly an airplane, drive over a bridge, go to war, or submit to surgery if he or she knew the designer of the airplane, the bridge, the battle plan, or the procedure worked solely from personal experience or "gut feel?"

The glaring exception: the world of competitive strategy. Strategists have had no choice but to rely on experience, on gut feel, on instinct, on conventional wisdom, on fads, on anecdotes.

We haven't had the competitive-strategy equivalent of wind tunnels, CAD/CAM software, or double-blind experiments. We've had to make do with tools borrowed from other disciplines: spreadsheets, for example, which are enormously valuable in many business areas but which are poorly suited for the dynamics, complexities, and uncertainties of competitive strategy.

We need new tools to help us formulate and test competitive strategies. These tools should understand the problems that strategists face:

- Competitors react to your moves, and you react to theirs. Your performance depends in part on their behavior. A competitive-strategy tool should incorporate this interplay, the very essence of the marketplace.

- Customers make purchase decisions using their perceptions of the relative quality and relative price offered by the firms competing in a market, tempered by their loyalty, their awareness of what's available, and the ability of those firms to satisfy their demand. A competitive-strategy tool should handle purchase decisions as adroitly as it handles financial statements.

- Picking head-to-head fights with competitors makes sense only when you know you can win. A competitive-strategy tool should help you assess your odds.

- Contingency plans and timely action become even more vital as customers' demands grow, product lifecycles shrink, technological progress accelerates, and competitors fight harder. A competitive-strategy tool should make powerful "what-if" analyses as easy as recalculating an income statement on a spreadsheet.

- Competitors' managers feel the same pressure to perform that you feel, so understanding what's likely to happen to them gives you information crucial to predicting how they're likely to behave. A competitive-strategy tool should report what happens to your competitors to help you see your market — and your actions — from their perspective.

- The "rules of the game" have changed in industry after industry. A competitive-strategy tool should make intelligent use of your knowledge of your markets and your competitors; it should not blindly extrapolate the historical patterns that are obsolete under the new rules.

And, of course, a competitive-strategy tool should be custom-tailored to your business' environment. No single battle plan will defeat every enemy; there is no magic strategy that will work for every business.

ValueWar is such a tool.

We call it **Value**War because competition centers on the quality/price combination — that is, product *value* — that competing businesses offer to their customers.

We call it Value**War** to stress the interactive nature of the strategies that the software simulates. ValueWar captures the ways that your actions influence your competitors' behavior, and that their actions influence yours.

ValueWar projects financial and strategic performance for each business it simulates. You can observe these measures for each competitor over the 20 quarters, or periods, in ValueWar's five-year outlook.

A tool has value only if it gets used. We designed ValueWar to be informative, responsive, colorful, and even fun, so that you and your colleagues will use it.

Does your competitive-strategy process:
√ Evaluate many alternatives?
√ Test competitors' reactions to your moves?
√ Seek good strategies, not precise forecasts?
√ Assume the past may not predict the future?
√ Look beyond an accounting view of the business?
√ Integrate customer needs with financial results?

Competitive strategies in ValueWar

Competitive strategies must aim simultaneously in two directions: outside and inside the company. ValueWar uses "market strategies" for the outward-focused aspects of competitive strategy and "operations strategies" for the inward-focused aspects. You select market and operations strategies for your business (and your competitors'), and ValueWar calculates how your performance (and theirs) evolves over the next five years.

Your business competes on the basis of the quality[1] and price your offer your customers, relative to what your competitors offer. Your market strategy determines when, how, and how fast you change your quality and price, and your competitors' market strategies determine changes to their quality and price. ValueWar simulates a wide range of market strategies that businesses employ in real life to help you select a path that will work well for you.

Your business' ability to compete also depends your operations strategy, which covers its cost structure, its speed of action, the costs it incurs or the savings it reaps from improving quality and enhancing productivity, and so on. ValueWar can express a broad range of operations strategies through the factors that describe how your business (and its competitors) operate.

Strategy Analysis with ValueWar uses the term "strategy" to refer to both market strategies and operations strategies.

ValueWar lets you select market strategies via the strategy menu and "non-strategy moves". ValueWar lets you specify operations strategies via the numbers you enter in the calibration process; you test those operations strategies via "scenarios", as described below and in Chapter 6 of the *Tutorial* section of this book.

If you have the ValueWar Calibrator software, you can set up and run ValueWar simulations on your markets: you can use all the market strategies, and you can specify and simulate operations strategies. The demonstration version of ValueWar lets you work with market strategies for a sample market.

---

[1] We take a very broad view of "quality." To ValueWar — and to real-life customers — quality is everything that the customer assesses in making a purchase decision. Quality covers not just product or service performance but also image, warranties, reputation, convenience, and so on. This view of quality is very important for competitive strategy; we encourage you to call to discuss it.

Enormous flexibility, enormous power

ValueWar's enormous flexibility lets you test performance far more easily and under far more circumstances than you can with conventional techniques. For example, you can compare performance under business-as-usual assumptions, to performance with minor, non-disruptive changes, to performance after major, paradigm-breaking revolutions. You can compare performance with your best guesses of competitors' future behavior to performance after surprise moves on their part. You can compare performance in different market segments. You can compare performance under expected market conditions to performance with unexpected blips, slumps, or changes in customer preferences.

When strategies confront each other in the ValueWar simulations, they demonstrate remarkably realistic competitive behavior. For example, some market strategies lead to price wars, others lead to highly segmented markets, and still others lead to races to out-do competitors' quality. And, as you'd expect, those strategies will work better for some competitors than others, due to differences in their operations strategies and capabilities.

Multiple scenarios for strategy analysis

You use ValueWar "scenarios" to describe strategic choices, market conditions, the initial positions of the competitors in that market, and the range of actions that the competitors can take. Your scenario descriptions control your ValueWar simulations.

For example, one scenario factor is market growth rate. If a scenario has a growth rate of 10%, then market demand will grow at a 10% compound annual growth rate under that scenario. Another scenario might have a -5% growth rate, reflecting a declining market.

The factors control the simulations as you'd expect. For example, if the businesses in a market are experiencing steady or shrinking demand, they're unlikely to add new capacity, while those in rapidly growing markets are almost certain to need capacity additions. The changes in capacity in turn affect costs, profits, and other results.

Thus, by setting appropriate values for ValueWar's factors, ValueWar can be made to realistically simulate markets with totally different characteristics. And, by using multiple scenarios, you can test your strategic options with different strategies, in different segments, or under different assumptions about your market and competitive position.

Here are a few strategies and market conditions you can test with ValueWar scenarios:

- By changing the market growth rate, you can simulate strategies under fast, slow, or expected growth. Markets can also be seasonal, cyclical, or both.
- By using different values for quality sensitivity and price sensitivity, you can simulate customers being more or less sensitive to changes in quality or price; that is, quality-sensitive or price-sensitive markets.

- By specifying various costs (or benefits) for improving quality, you can simulate which methods of improving quality are likely to work best. You can even simulate competing against businesses whose costs of quality differ from yours.

- By setting the factors for the time it takes for businesses to react to their competitors' actions, you can simulate dealing with fast-moving, aggressive competitors, or slow-moving, complacent competitors, or some of each.

- By controlling the factors for customer loyalty, customer disloyalty, and the time it takes for customers to perceive changes in quality and price, you can simulate stubborn or inattentive customers versus trendy or knowledgeable customers. You can also simulate customers with high switching costs or low switching costs.

The multiple-scenario capability is a major benefit of ValueWar simulations. Multiple scenarios let you see whether and when your strategic decisions ought to change. You can even see where better market or competitive data would help you improve your strategic decisions.

For example, if you find that your business's strategy works equally well whether or not the market grows at the rate you expect, then you don't have to worry much about precise forecasts of market growth; the rate of growth doesn't change your decisions. On the other hand, if you find that the degree of price sensitivity *does* affect the strategy you should pursue, then you know you should measure price sensitivity carefully and you know that you should consider a shift in strategy if price sensitivity changes over time.

The ValueWar Calibrator

You use the ValueWar Calibrator™ software to describe your scenarios. The Calibrator lets you enter whatever factor values best model your business's market, operations, and competitors.

With the Calibrator, you can create as many scenarios as you like and change them as often as you like. Thus, the Calibrator lets you quickly and easily update your ValueWar analyses as conditions in your market change or as you encounter opportunities to induce changes within your business. For example, you would calibrate new scenarios if:

- A small but aggressive competitor introduces an unexpected new product with extraordinarily high quality or unusually low price.

- You want to test the potential upside benefits against the possible downside risks of changing your make/buy decisions (i.e., your vertical integration).

- You discover one or more new options for improving the perceived quality of your products and services, and those options have different costs.

- Your market research suggests that your market may be less (or more) price sensitive than you thought.

Some questions you can address with ValueWar

- Should your business raise or cut quality and price? When? How much?
- Should your business improve quality by upgrading workers' skills, by using higher-precision equipment, or by buying better-quality subassemblies?
- How should your business respond to competitors' quality and price moves?
- Can improving your strategic reaction times improve your bottom line?
- Must your business trade profits for growth?
- Is it better to go head-to-head with a competitor or to find separate niches?
- Does it pay to "cheat" by sneaking in a temporary price cut?
- Does it pay to retaliate against a competitor who cuts price?

Summary of features

This list summarizes key ValueWar features to illustrate its flexibility and friendliness.

Strategies	• Select from a variety of market strategies for each competitor • Switch from one strategy to another in any period • Override strategies with specific quality/price changes in any period
Scenarios	• Execute operations strategies under various market/competitive environments
Sensitivity analyses	• See how much your business's performance depends on your assumptions • Test all strategies for one business to see which performs best • Find out if competitors are more or less vulnerable than your business • See what factors have the most effect on your business's performance
Animation	• "Animate" ValueWar's graphic display of your market to watch it evolve
Reports	• Print reports for detailed analysis and reference • Export ValueWar data for word processors, spreadsheets, or charting programs
Help	• Display on-screen, context-sensitive lists of available analyses • Obtain on-screen definitions of all ValueWar data • Show detailed on-screen descriptions of strategies and scenarios

ValueWar services

Companies and universities use ValueWar in a number of ways.

The ValueWar software and calibration process help organize the strategy-development process. They ask the critical questions and provide a tool for analyzing the answers.

ValueWar "war games" customized to specific businesses are highly effective for helping management teams achieve a common understanding of their competitive situation and of their strategic options. Such exercises also help break outdated paradigms and help familiarize managers with their competitors' objectives and capabilities.

Executive-education seminars using ValueWar offer companies an interactive, insightful, thought-provoking way to learn state-of-the-art concepts in competitive strategy. These seminars can use existing case studies or, for optimum learning in a corporate setting, they can use case studies drawn from the company's own businesses.

Computer requirements

ValueWar runs on IBM-compatible personal computers. It requires a color monitor and 640K of RAM. A hard disk and a math coprocessor are recommended but not required.

As Arnold Palmer says, "The more I practice, the luckier I get."
ValueWar lets you practice your strategy before you play for keeps.

STRATEGY ANALYSIS WITH VALUEWAR

VALUEWAR
Tutorial

1 Installing ValueWar

The computer

ValueWar will run on any IBM-compatible personal computer with a color monitor.[1] It can use but doesn't require a hard disk, printer, or math coprocessor (but see "A note on speed" and "A note on printing" below). You can even run ValueWar on a Macintosh equipped with a PC emulator called SoftPC Professional™, from Insignia Solutions.

Almost all PCs have sufficient memory (RAM) for ValueWar.[2] However, some ValueWar features may need more RAM than your PC contains. If that occurs, ValueWar will tell you that it can't do some analyses. Please also see "A note on memory," below.

Copying ValueWar onto your hard disk

You can run ValueWar from the floppy disk on which it comes. However, using a hard disk will make ValueWar start up more quickly and save reports more quickly.

If you want to use a hard disk, you must copy several files from the ValueWar floppy disk. You should copy all files whose names bear the prefix "VW"; that is, copy VW.*. ValueWar is not copy protected, so you can just use the DOS COPY command.

ValueWar must be able to access all VW files simultaneously. In technical terms, you must place them in the same subdirectory, and that subdirectory must be the current subdirectory when you run ValueWar.

Here is a typical installation sequence. It assumes that you have a hard disk in your PC, that your PC is turned on and running, and that you have put the ValueWar diskette in floppy-disk drive A. You should see the C:> prompt that says you're working with your hard-disk drive. (If your computer is set up with hard-disk directories such as drive D or E, you can use one of those drives instead of drive C.)

---

[1] ValueWar will run with shade-of-grey screens, but it may look ugly and you may not be able to read all of the screens.
[2] It is difficult for ValueWar to detect certain conditions of insufficient memory. If ValueWar seems to behave oddly, try increasing the memory available to it by unloading "memory resident" programs. Please contact us if you have questions or problems.

Your commands	Comments
CD \	Ensures you're starting with the top-level subdirectory. There should be a space between the "CD" and the "\."
MD VW	Creates a "subdirectory" for ValueWar. You can call the subdirectory anything you want.
CD VW	Makes the ValueWar subdirectory the current directory
COPY A:VW.*	Copies the ValueWar files to the subdirectory. Use the command COPY A:*.* if you want to copy the ValueWar READ.ME file too (see below).

Late-breaking information

Your ValueWar disk might contain a file called READ.ME. If it does, that file will have information not present in this book. You should read it before you proceed further; just enter the DOS command TYPE A:READ.ME to read it. (If the file's contents don't fit on your screen, try the command TYPE A:READ.ME | MORE. The "|" character is the vertical bar located above the (ENTER) key on most PC keyboards.)

If information in the READ.ME file conflicts with information in this book, you should believe the READ.ME file.

A note on speed

Because of the large number of calculations it performs, ValueWar will run considerably faster on an AT than on a PC or an XT. Running ValueWar on an 80486-based computer provides nearly instantaneous response.

Much of ValueWar's interactive nature will be lost if you have to wait for calculations, so we strongly recommend that you use ValueWar in a fast computer or in one with a math coprocessor chip (e.g., an 8087, 80287, or 80387). Most math coprocessors cost about $100. An AT-class (80286) computer with a coprocessor runs ValueWar as fast, or even faster, than a 386-based computer without a coprocessor.

Aside from convenience, *boosting calculating speed can improve your analyses*. You're much more likely to test several scenarios if you don't have to wait for the computer to think. A standard PC without a math chip takes about a minute for ValueWar's normal calculations. An AT-compatible with an 80287 math coprocessor takes about two seconds. A 486DX-equipped PC will run the numbers almost instantaneously.

A note on memory

ValueWar's appetite for memory (RAM) depends on the analyses you ask it to perform and on the number of scenarios available for analysis. The demonstration version of ValueWar comes with two sets of scenarios; you can choose among them depending on whether your computer has plenty of memory, or not so much memory, available.

If you run ValueWar as described in this *Tutorial*, you'll automatically get the larger set of scenarios. This set contains ten scenarios that demonstrate a wide variety of scenarios. You'll get this set of scenarios by running ValueWar with the command VW.

If you run ValueWar with the command VW SHORT, then you'll have access to six scenarios, a subset of the ten. The smaller set is less demanding on your computer's memory. Note: The ValueWar software itself is identical whether you run the smaller or larger set of scenarios. The only thing that's different in the two approaches is how many varieties of markets you can explore.

Note to users of the ValueWar Calibrator

When you use the ValueWar Calibrator to devise your own scenarios, you control the number and content of the scenarios. In addition, you can have multiple sets of scenarios. If you create multiple sets of scenarios, each in its own scenario file, you would use a command similar to the one shown above to access the desired set of scenarios. For example, if you create a set of scenarios in a file called CONSUMER.PAR, you would use those scenarios with ValueWar by entering this command: VW CONSUMER.

You can determine how much memory your computer has available for ValueWar by typing the DOS command MEM just before you run ValueWar. It will report, along with other technical points of interest, how much memory is available for programs in the line labeled "largest executable program" or something similar. ValueWar requires that that number be at least 560,000 (560K) or so to run all its analyses.[1] You may need to pay particular attention to available memory if you run ValueWar via the "DOS prompt" that you open while using Microsoft Windows.

Technical note: ValueWar does not require (or access) expanded or extended memory. It uses only conventional DOS memory.

---

[1] ValueWar will run with less memory. However, it may have to recalculate certain analyses more frequently, which can be a minor inconvenience. If available memory is very tight, then ValueWar may be unable to run certain analyses.

A note on printing

ValueWar can print most of its analyses to whatever printer you have connected to your PC. (If you try to print an analysis that ValueWar can't print, nothing bad will happen; ValueWar will simply tell you that it's unable to satisfy your request.) ValueWar can print to laser, dot-matrix, and other kinds of printers, including (in most cases) printers connected to your PC via a network.

If you run into printing difficulty, you can work around the trouble by saving your ValueWar analyses to a file (via the "save" command) and then printing the file by your usual printing commands after you've exited from ValueWar.

Chapter 3 of the *Tutorial* describes the ValueWar printing and saving commands.

ValueWar can handle two special printing situations:

- *Preventing double-spaced printouts.* Some printers double-space their output with ValueWar. To prevent this behavior, run ValueWar with the /SINGLESPACE switch. You can abbreviate this switch to /SING.

  Example: VW /SINGLESPACE

- *Preventing extra blank pages.* Some printers eject an extra page at the end of ValueWar printouts. To prevent this behavior, run ValueWar with the /NOFORMFEED switch. You can abbreviate this switch to /NOF.

  Example: VW /NOFORMFEED

You can combine either or both of these switches with the ValueWar command to use other scenario files. The commands can appear in any order after the VW part.

  Example, with scenario file CONSUMER.PAR: VW CONSUMER /SING /NOF

2 Basic ValueWar

Chapter 2, *Basic ValueWar*, demonstrates ValueWar's analyses and options with a sample analysis, built up piece by piece. Subsequent chapters focus on strategy instead of the software, adding great detail to the analysis that this chapter begins.

This chapter assumes that you have installed the ValueWar software. See Chapter 1, *Installing ValueWar*, if you have not. You'll get the most value out of the *Tutorial* if you run ValueWar as you read.

The *Tutorial* uses a simple case analysis to help you get familiar with ValueWar. Chapter 6 of the *Tutorial* discusses ValueWar analysis for more-realistic business situations.

ValueWar versions

Although this book uses ValueWar version 1.64, it also applies pretty well to earlier versions. You may get somewhat different results if you use a version other than 1.64 — and you will certainly get different results if you use a version customized for your business — but the concepts and interpretations presented here also pertain to the other versions.

Typefaces

This book uses several typographical styles. When a word appears in **bold type**, you're seeing the first occurrence of ValueWar jargon. Keys you press on your keyboard during the *Tutorial* usually show up in a special typeface: (HOME), (←), (TAB), (ENTER). Letters or phrases you type also appear in that typeface: (A), (123), and (?) mean you should type "A," "123," and the question mark.

Starting up

Enter the command (VW). After a second or two, you should see ValueWar's **logo screen**.[1] The bottom line on the screen will alternate between identifying ValueWar's copyright and asking you to press any key to proceed. Please press any key.

---

[1] If you don't see the logo screen, or if you see an error message, then something went wrong (obviously!). ValueWar will probably issue a reasonably clear announcement to tell you what happened. As always, please feel free to contact us with questions.

To help you use the "arrow" keys, ValueWar will turn off the (NUM LOCK) function on your keyboard. If (NUM LOCK) was turned on when you started ValueWar, ValueWar will turn it back on when you exit ValueWar.

Selecting a scenario

The logo screen will vanish, to be replaced by the first of several menus. You use the **scenario menu** to select a scenario for ValueWar's simulations. You can simulate results under different scenarios by invoking the scenario menu later on.

Note to users of the ValueWar Calibrator

You can devise different scenarios to simulate different operations strategies, market environments, customer preferences, etc. See Chapter 6 and the *Reference* section.

```
Please select a scenario for your
ValueWar analyses

a: Horse race

b: Capital horse race

c: Hi-tech horse race

d: Recession horse race

e: Price-horse race

f: Quality-horse race

g: Seasonal horse race

h: Loyal-horse race

i: Eligible-horse race

j: Reacting-horse race
```

The scenario menu with the ValueWar demo. You'll see fewer scenarios if you run the "short" demo; see Chapter 1.

ValueWar starts by highlighting the top line in the scenario menu, labeled "Horse race."[1] You don't know yet what these scenarios are, of course; look at the bottom line of the screen for directions on how to get some help.

Notice that the bottom line of the ValueWar screen says you can use the (F2) key for a definition.[2] Press (F2) now. ValueWar will pop up a window that describes the Horse-race scenario. The bottom of the screen asks you to press any key when you're ready to proceed. When you're ready, please press a key.

Note that ValueWar says you can use the (F1) key for help. It's different from (F2): (F2) describes the scenario, and (F1) offers, among other things, detail about each scenario. Feel free to peruse the help features, but we'll cover them in Chapter 3.

The bottom line mentions that you can use the (↑) and (↓) keys to point to items in the menu. Press (↑) and (↓) a few times now. You'll see the highlight move from scenario to scenario. Nothing bad will happen if you press (↓) when you're at the bottom of the list or (↑) when you're

---

[1] The scenarios in the demonstration version of ValueWar were designed to depict "generic" business situations. Of course, ValueWar scenarios can be calibrated to model specific markets for real-life strategy analysis. See the *Reference* section of this book for more details.
[2] The bottom line of the ValueWar screen always contains tips on how to proceed.

at the top. As with most PC software, you can also use the (HOME) and (PGUP) keys to move immediately to the top of the list, and the (END) and (PGDN) keys to skip to the bottom.

Please move the highlight back to "Horse race." As the bottom line indicates, pressing (ENTER) (shown as (RETURN) or (↵) on some keyboards) will select that scenario for your simulations. Press (ENTER) to tell ValueWar to use Horse race.

Selecting market strategies

Since you selected a scenario, ValueWar replaces the scenario menu with the first **strategy menu**. You'll see this menu four times, once for each of four competitors. (Important: You can alter the strategy menu to use different strategies. For details, please see the *Strategy Reference* in the *Reference* section of this book.)

```
Business: Amalgamated, Inc.
Scenario: Horse race

Please select a market strategy
for periods 0 through 20
┌─────────────────────────────┐
│ a: Don't change Q or P      │
└─────────────────────────────┘
  b: Highest Q and P

  c: Highest Q, steady P

  d: Steady Q, lowest P

  e: Raise Q and P

  f: Raise Q, lag P

  g: Lowest Q and P

  h: P by supply/demand

  i: Highest Q, average P

  j: Match mkt average

  k: Match #1's Q and P

  l: Beat #1's price

  m: Lead Q and P up

  n: Follow success

  o: Tit for best tat
```

The strategy menu with the demonstration version of ValueWar looks like this

ValueWar uses color codes to distinguish the four businesses, so the strategy menus are color-coded. The first strategy menu, for a business dubbed Amalgamated, shows the highlight line in yellow.

The strategy menus work like the scenario menu. You can use keys such as (↑), (↓), and (HOME) to move the highlight. You use the (ENTER) key to select the strategy on which the highlight is resting. You can get help and definitions with the (F1) and (F2) keys.

Now is a good time to get familiar with some of ValueWar's strategies. Please move the highlight and press (F2) on one or more of the strategies.[1] The definitions tell you how each strategy causes competitors to behave. Differences between strategies are subtle but important, as we'll see when we explore ValueWar's analyses in Chapter 5.

Please move the highlight to the "Highest Q and P" strategy for Amalgamated, then press (ENTER) to indicate that Amalgamated will follow that strategy. This strategy tells Amalgamated to observe its competitors' quality and prices and then adjust its own — within its constraints — to target the high-quality, high-price segment of the market.

---

[1] ValueWar market strategies cover a wide range of strategic options. If you need to model other strategic behavior, new ValueWar strategies can be added or current ones modified. Please contact us for details.

Having chosen a strategy for Amalgamated, ValueWar shows you the strategy menu again, this time for BigBiz. Note that the menu says you're working on BigBiz, a message reinforced by the cyan (light blue) highlight for the menu.

BigBiz's managers think that they'll get the biggest payoff by offering top-notch quality while holding the line on price. That is, they want to provide high "value" for their customers. So, press ⊕ twice, then (ENTER), to select "Highest Q, steady P" for BigBiz.

Now you're on the strategy menu for Consolidated, with a magenta (purple) highlight. Consolidated's managers think they'll make the most money by going for volume, and they think price is the key to maximizing volume, so they want to cut prices. They also think they'll maintain their margins by shaving their quality.

The strategy for Consolidated is "Lowest Q and P." You could press ⊕ six times, then (ENTER), but ValueWar's menus offer a quicker way. Each item in the menus starts with a letter; you can press that letter to immediately select that item. (You can use this technique on any ValueWar menu with this alphabetical arrangement.) Please press (G) — you don't have to press (ENTER) — to select "Lowest Q and P" for Consolidated.

Now you're on the last competitor, Diversified, colored red. Diversified pays strict attention to its competitors. In addition, it's not concerned with grabbing a market segment; it just wants to make a buck. Diversified likes the "Follow success" strategy, which would have them do whatever seems to work for others in their market.

> Strive for the quality and price position attained by whichever competitor had the highest profits in the last period. If a business following this strategy itself had the highest profits, it will maintain its position.
>
> A business following this strategy watches only those competitors who are large enough to be "noticed," as controlled by a scenario factor. If none is large enough, then the business following this strategy will not change its quality or price.

This is the definition you'll see if you press (F2) while highlighting the "Follow success" strategy

You could press (n) or (N) to select this strategy for Diversified. But say you want to get a definition of "Follow success" first; how does ValueWar define "success"? The fastest way to move to this strategy without selecting it: press (PGDN) to move to the bottom of the list, then ⊕. Now you can press (F2) to learn that success means profits. Satisfied with this definition, you can press a key to remove the definition, then (ENTER) to select the strategy.

You've selected strategies for all four competitors. ValueWar removes the strategy menus and starts to crunch numbers.

ValueWar "views"

ValueWar offers you a series of **views** on the analyses you run. The views present ValueWar's calculations in a variety of formats that were designed to highlight particular issues.

ValueWar shows the outline of the value view immediately after you select all your strategies, then superimposes a simple graph to let you know that it's performing the calculations for the simulation you specified. Depending on your computer, the calculations may take anywhere from a second to a minute.

ValueWar begins with the value view; you can change the view later with a single keystroke.

Here is a list of ValueWar's views. Don't worry if some of the nomenclature doesn't make sense now. We will discuss each view as we proceed through the *Tutorial*.

View	Contents
Value	Graph quality, price, and market share
Graph	Show the current data in graph form
Data history	Show all periods of the current data
Competition	Summarize competitive performance
Financial snapshot	Show financial data for the current period
Profit and loss	Summarize financial performance
Scenario test	Show sensitivity of results to scenario
Strategy test	Show sensitivity of results to strategy

When its calculations are done, ValueWar removes the bar graph and fills in the value view. We'll introduce the parts of the view one at a time, showing you how to manipulate and interpret the information in each part.

As always, ValueWar puts a line at the bottom of the screen that contains a few key hints and reminders.

The value view

The value view contains several parts.

The value map

The main section of the value view is the **value map**. The chart, located in the upper left corner of the screen, indicates each business's market share and its quality and price (relative to the quality and price of its competitors).

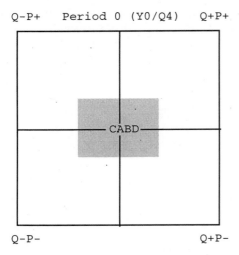

Q-P+   Period 0 (Y0/Q4)   Q+P+

CABD

Q-P-   Q+P-

*The ValueWar value map at the
start of the Horse-race scenario*

ValueWar graphs **relative quality** along the horizontal axis and **relative price** along the vertical. The center line on each axis corresponds to 100%, which means "equivalent to competitors." The area to the left of the center line on relative quality indicates quality worse than the market average, and the area to the right indicates quality superior to the average. Similarly, the upper half of the relative-price axis represents higher-than-average prices, and the half below the line represents prices below the average.

Each competitor is identified by its color and one-letter ID. (Amalgamated is "A" on yellow, BigBiz is "B" on cyan, etc.) ValueWar graphs the four points for the four competitors according to their relative quality and relative price. At the beginning of the Horse-race scenario, all the competitors charge the same price for equivalent-quality products, so each has 100% relative quality and relative price. You should see all four points near the centerline (which indicates 100%) of the two axes. ValueWar adjusts the locations at which the IDs are displayed to make sure that all four show up.

ValueWar puts each competitor's ID inside a color-coded rectangle whose size is proportional to the competitor's market share. At the beginning of Horse race, the competitors have the same shares and the same position on the value map, so you can see only one rectangle; the others are "underneath" it. ValueWar draws the largest rectangles first, so it doesn't hide small-share businesses under larger competitors. In this case, though, the four rectangles are the same size, so you can't see the bottom three.

ValueWar indicates the **current period** at the top of the value map; that is, the period the chart is displaying. You should see "Period 0 (Y0/Q4)," which means that the graph shows the state of the market at the initial position (period 0), before any of the strategies take effect. The initial position corresponds to year 0, quarter 4 … in other words, the quarter before Y1/Q1, the period in which the simulation begins.

You can use "arrow" keys to change the current period. The ⊕ key moves to the next period, and ⊕ moves to the prior; (HOME) moves to the first period, and (END) to the last; (PGUP) moves to the first period of the [prior] year, and (PGDN) to the first period of the next year. As you'll see in Chapter 3, all these keys are listed in on-screen help that you can summon while you're running ValueWar. You don't have to memorize the keys.

Press ⊕. Here's what you should see:

- The current period at the top of the map changes from period 0 to period 1.

- Amalgamated ("A") moves to the upper right, which indicates that its quality and price both rose, relative to its competitors' quality and price.

- BigBiz ("B") shifts to the right because its relative quality rose, while its relative price held steady.

- Consolidated ("C") migrates southwest because its relative quality and its relative price both dropped.

- Diversified ("D") moves left just a little. Its relative quality slipped a bit, and its relative price stayed at 100%.

Experiment with these keys. You can see a graphic evolution of the market.

We'll discuss how to interpret the strategic changes, as well as ValueWar's "animation" feature, in Chapter 3. For now, please press (HOME) to move back to period 0.

The strategy window

At the lower right of the value view you'll see ValueWar's **strategy window**. The strategy window shows the market strategy each competitor used in each period.

In period 0, ValueWar displays "Initial position" in the strategy window for each competitor. That's what you should see now. If you don't, please press (HOME).

```
A   Amalgamated, Inc.

    Highest Q and P

B   BigBiz Corporation

    Highest Q, steady P

C   Consolidated Company

    Lowest Q and P

D   Diversified Limited

    Follow success
```

This is what the strategy window looks like in period 1

In subsequent periods, ValueWar displays the name of the strategy that you choose for each competitor. (We'll show later how to change strategies.) Press ⊕ to change the current period to period 1. Now you should see the names of the strategies you entered. The strategy window stays up-to-date with the rest of the value view.

The supply/demand window

Directly above the strategy window perches the **supply/demand window**. This window indicates the market's unit capacity (supply) and unit demand for the current period. These figures represent totals across all four competitors.

In period 1, the combined capacity of the four competitors is 50,000 units. Total customer demand for their products was 40,688 units. The market has more supply than demand; overall capacity utilization is just over 80% (utilization = demand ÷ supply). Of course, the figures for individual competitors may show very different values.

As you use the arrow keys to change the current period, the supply/demand window changes too. It stays synchronized with the rest of the value view.

The data window

Finally, ValueWar draws the **data window** at the upper right of the value view. In this window you can see the data that ValueWar calculates for all four competitors.

Per	Absolute price				
0	1.00			1.00
1	1.02			1.00
2	1.04			1.00
3	1.06	A	B	1.00
0	1.00	C	D	1.00
1	0.98			1.00
2	0.96			1.02
3	0.95			1.04

The data window for periods 0 through 3. Absolute price is the current data. We'll discuss the data on the next page.

The data window shows one data value at a time (the **current data**), listing the results for four quarters (one year) for all four competitors. If you've entered keystrokes as directed so far, you should see the label "Absolute price" at the top of the data window, which indicates that the current data is absolute price. The left side of the window indicates that you're seeing the current data for periods 0 through 3. Within the window you can see four sets of numbers, which are the absolute prices charged by each of the competitors for the first four periods.

You can use the ← and → keys to switch the data displayed in the data window. Press →; you should see different numbers and the label "Relative price." Press → again, and you'll get "Absolute quality."

The list of data goes through an endless loop. If you press → enough times, you'll get back to absolute price. You can also move immediately to the beginning of the loop by holding down the (CTRL) key and pressing ←, and to the end of the loop — cumulative profits — with (CTRL)-→.

You can ask ValueWar to define whatever data is currently on display in the data window. As before, press the (F2) key to get a definition. You might want to take a moment now to get familiar with ValueWar's data and their definitions by switching the data window and getting definitions.

Like the other windows, the data window stays synchronized with the others in the value view. Because it covers four periods, the data window won't necessarily look any different when you change the current period. However, the data window is guaranteed always to contain the current period.

For now, we'll stay with the value view. Chapter 3 will introduce the others.

Highlights of the value view

The value view — in particular the value map — provides a great deal of information in a form you can absorb quickly. At a glance you can see how competitors' market shares have changed by observing the size of their rectangles on the map; switching from period to period makes their successes and failures quite apparent. You can also see the market position that each competitor has staked out by seeing the location of their rectangles. Competitors ascending toward the upper right corner are going for the premium combination of high quality and high price, whereas those gravitating toward the lower left are striving for the low-quality, low-price, economy-minded customer. Using ValueWar's animation feature makes market evolution dramatically apparent.

Interpreting competitors' actions

In this section we'll explore what the four competitors did to change their positions from period 0 to period 1. We'll focus on four factors: absolute and relative price, and absolute and relative quality. (Chapters 4 and 5 will analyze competitive behavior and performance in much more detail.) Please use the arrow keys freely to shift the display among those data, as well as between periods 0 and 1.

To start, please set the display to absolute price in the data window and period 1 in the value view. To do so, press these keys:

- (CTRL)-(←) to select absolute price.
- (HOME) to move to period 0.
- (↓) to advance to period 1.

In the data window, you'll see that Amalgamated increased its price from 1.00 to 1.02 between periods 0 and 1. It increased its price because its strategy — note the strategy window — calls for it to try to have both quality and price higher than those of its competitors.[1]

---

[1] Various constraints and factors in each scenario determine the feasible rates of change in quality and price, the maximum total change in quality and price, the degree of differentiation

BigBiz and Diversified held their prices at 1.00, but for different reasons. BigBiz's strategy (Highest Q, steady P) means that it'll change its quality but it won't change its price. Diversified, on the other hand, wants to "Follow success," and in period 0 the most successful business — Diversified doesn't care that all four were the "most" successful — had a price of 1.00.

Consolidated cut its price to 0.98, in accordance with its strategy of going for the lowest quality and price.

Changes in relative price mirror the changes in absolute price from period 0 to 1, because the competitors start from the same position in the Horse-race scenario. (Press ⊙ if you want to see relative price in the data window.)

Amalgamated and BigBiz both improved their absolute quality, going from 70 to 72, in accordance with the strategies they're pursuing. (Press ⊙ again to shift the data window to absolute quality.) Going for the low road, Consolidated cut its quality. Diversified held its quality to 70, since that's what the most successful business did in period 0.

Changes in relative quality (press ⊙ again) don't precisely match the changes in absolute quality … an important distinction, because it's *relative* quality and *relative* price that determine changes in market share. Amalgamated and BigBiz went up, as did their absolute quality, and Consolidated went down, as did its absolute quality. However, Diversified's relative quality declined, even though it made no change at all in its absolute quality! The reason: the average of the market rose, due to Amalgamated and BigBiz's quality war, and so Diversified isn't as good as the average any more.

Interpreting supply and demand

Supply and demand depend on a number of factors, including the underlying market growth rate, the time it takes competitors to add capacity, and elasticities of demand due to changes in overall quality and price. If, for example, the market grows very quickly, demand may outstrip supply until competitors can build new capacity. As another example, market demand will drop if competitors choose strategies that result in prices rising significantly.

In the Horse-race scenario, basic market growth runs at 6% per annum, so we'd expect market demand to grow from 40,688 in period 1 to 43,129 in period 5. However, the market average price didn't change from period 1 to 5, whereas average quality went from 70 to 76. Improved quality stimulates additional demand, which caused total demand in period 5 to exceed 43,129. We'll discuss in Chapter 3 how you can review the factors that drive supply and demand.

---

that a business can tolerate before it's forced to respond to a competitor, and so on. These factors are calibrated to match particular markets for real analysis. See the *Reference* section.

Looking at subsequent periods

You can understand competitors' behavior in subsequent periods in the same way you did between 0 and 1. For example, you'll see that Amalgamated and BigBiz constantly try to outdo each other's quality (until they hit a maximum-total-change constraint in period 13)[1], because both their strategies want to attain the highest quality position. Another example: Diversified emulates Amalgamated because Amalgamated reports the highest profits in every period. (Are those profits unrealistically high? Maybe, for some industries; maybe not in others. If you think they are, you can manipulate strategies, as we'll show later, to make the competitors shift gears. If you have the ValueWar Calibrator, you can change some of the scenario factors, such as price sensitivity, to reflect different assumptions about the market.)

You can contrast competitors' performance that accrue from their different strategies. By shifting the current period and the current data with the arrow keys, you can find:

- Amalgamated loses more than 20% of its unit share, ending up as the smallest competitor. However, it's also very profitable. It never incurs the extra expense of building regular capacity. It's at a cost disadvantage, but it has won a segment that's willing to pay for its high-quality products.

- BigBiz gains the most share and adds as much capacity as its constraints allow. Despite its soaring sales and accumulated experience, its variable costs rise somewhat, due to the cost of improving quality.

- Consolidated captures the low quality, low price segment without a battle. It's forced to raise quality eventually, because its competitors get so far ahead that Consolidated would no longer be selling a viable product. Consolidated runs its plants at 89% utilization even after adding as much capacity as it can … and ends up with the lowest profits.

- Diversified promptly and successfully follows Amalgamated's strategy. Diversified's cumulative profits are less than 5% behind Amalgamated's. If another competitor with a different strategy was jockeying with Amalgamated for highest profits, though, Diversified might have ended up seesawing between strategies, possibly to its own detriment.

You can see that after five years (20 periods) BigBiz and Consolidated have come to the end of their capacity: they're running 89% or more capacity utilization, and they can't add any more capacity. Further growth in the market will cause customers to buy from Amalgamated and Diversified, since they have (or can add) the capacity, which will cause their profits to ascend even higher. At full utilization, perhaps BigBiz and Consolidated should consider raising prices.

Even though these points barely scratch the surface of a full analysis, they raise new questions that you could tackle with the techniques you've already used in ValueWar:

- What would happen if BigBiz challenged Amalgamated directly, by increasing its prices too?

---

[1] For more information on constraints, please see the *Reference* section of this book.

- What would happen if BigBiz switched to a strategy with higher prices after a couple of years had passed and it had gained lots of loyal customers with its dominant market share?

- What would happen if another competitor took Consolidated's approach? Would a price war result? Would it drag down just the combatants or would it ruin the whole market?

- What would happen if Diversified wanted to copy the biggest-share competitor, rather than the highest-profit competitor? Would Amalgamated be better off with the high-price segment to itself?

The chapters that follow will show how to operate ValueWar to address these and other questions. Chapter 5 explores one analytic thread in detail.

Shutting down

If you want to stop running ValueWar at this point, just press the (ESC) key a few times. The (ESC) key lets you cancel or exit from functions in ValueWar, and if you press it enough times, you will stop running ValueWar altogether.

You can, of course, restart ValueWar after you stop it. The remaining chapters of the *Tutorial* will tell you what stage of ValueWar analysis you should resume if you choose to stop ValueWar now.

Summary

In your first run through ValueWar, you've seen how to simulate a set of strategies under one scenario. You've seen how ValueWar calculates and displays the performance that each competitor attains with its strategy. You've seen how different strategies produce different results among competitors who started from identical positions.

Chapter 3 will introduce a number of new features. You'll see:

- How to access other views and create reports.
- How to "animate" the main screen.
- How to get more kinds of on-screen help.

Chapter 4 will present advanced analytic techniques. You'll see:

- How to play "what if" by changing strategies and scenarios.
- How to perform "non-strategy" moves.
- How to run sensitivity analyses.

3 More ValueWar Features

This chapter puts strategy analysis temporarily aside to demonstrate ValueWar's view, report, and "animate" features, as well as the remaining options in the help system. These features can make ValueWar analyses easier and more enjoyable to perform. Chapter 4, *Advanced ValueWar*, returns to ValueWar's business-strategy focus.

If you're running the ValueWar demo while you're going through the *Tutorial*, please set up the software so that you're where you'd be if you just finished Chapter 2:

Scenario	Horse race
View..................................	Value view
Amalgamated.....................	Highest Q and P
BigBiz	Highest Q, steady P
Consolidated	Lowest Q and P
Diversified	Follow success
Current data......................	Absolute price
Current period...................	0 (initial position)

Views

Views **show your ValueWar analyses from different perspectives**

ValueWar offers you a variety of ways that you can arrange and display the data that it calculates. These different displays, called **views**, highlight different strategic perspectives.

Unless you switch to another view, ValueWar automatically displays the value view. (You saw the value view in Chapter 2.) ValueWar has seven more views, which we will describe in a moment.[1] Each view is identified by name in the lower-left corner of the screen.

Switching among views

You can switch among ValueWar's views in two ways: by pressing keys that move from one view to another in an endless loop, or by pressing keys that immediately access a specific view.

---

[1] Two of the views are available after you tell ValueWar to run certain analyses. ValueWar will automatically skip unavailable views as you cycle through the view loop.

3/ More ValueWar Features

ValueWar's views are arranged in an endless loop of eight views. The first view is the value view. Pressing ⊕ moves to the second view; pressing ⊕ again moves to the third view, and so on through the remaining views. When you get to the last view, pressing ⊕ again moves you back to the value view. Pressing ⊖ works exactly the same way, except it moves backward.

If you prefer, you can press (CTRL)-(PGDN) instead of ⊕, and you can swap (CTRL)-(PGUP) for ⊖.

You can also access any view immediately by pressing the key assigned to that view. Here is a list of ValueWar's views and of the keys assigned to each one. (The views are shown in the order that they'll appear if you keep pressing ⊕.)

View	Direct key	Contents
Value	(SHIFT)-(F1)	Graph quality, price, & market share
Graph	(SHIFT)-(F2)	Show the current data in graph form
Data history	(SHIFT)-(F3)	Show all periods of the current data
Competition	(SHIFT)-(F4)	Summarize competitive performance
Financial snapshot	(SHIFT)-(F5)	Show financial data for current period
Profit and loss	(SHIFT)-(F6)	Summarize financial performance
Scenario test	(SHIFT)-(F7)	Show sensitivity to scenario
Strategy test	(SHIFT)-(F8)	Show sensitivity of results to strategy

Thus, to move immediately to the financial-snapshot view (regardless of the view currently displayed on your screen), hold down the (SHIFT) key and press (F5).

Some views show one factor at a time (for example, the data window shows one factor in the value view). When you switch from one view to another, ValueWar does its best to keep that same factor, during the same period, on the screen. But not all views display all factors, so ValueWar might occasionally highlight a new factor when you ask for a new view.

As described below, the ValueWar help system offers lists of the keys you press to change views.

> **Note:** The scenario-test and strategy-test views are not available until you ask ValueWar to calculate the corresponding sensitivity test. (In other words, you can't see the strategy-test view until you run the strategy-sensitivity test.) Running those tests requires just a single keystroke, as described later in this chapter. If you haven't run a test, ValueWar will politely refuse to display a view of the test, and it will remind you that you need to perform the analysis before you can see the results.

Saving and printing views

You can do all your analysis with the views on the screen, or you may want to refer later on to views you've generated. You can tell ValueWar to save or to print views that you produce. You can save a view to a file on your computer's disk, and you can print a view if your computer is connected to a printer.[1] Either way, you create a permanent record of the analysis you've performed.

The Ⓢ key saves a view. The Ⓟ key prints it.

It takes but a single keystroke to save or print a view.

- To save a view, press Ⓢ while the view is on the screen. ValueWar will save the view in a file named **VW.REP.** If you already have such a file, ValueWar will append the view to that file; it won't erase what you have already saved.[2]

- To print a view, press Ⓟ while the view is on the screen. You can interrupt the printing by pressing any key, as ValueWar reminds you with a message on the bottom of the screen. If ValueWar has any trouble printing the view, it will tell you what ails it and ask you to fix the problem. You can resume printing after fixing the problem.

You could use the ⒫ʳᵗˢᶜʳ⒭ key to print any view, but we urge you not to. One reason: ValueWar's printing feature produces more-attractive, easier-to-read results. A more-important reason: ValueWar inserts reference information (e.g., a list of the strategies that you ran) that doesn't show up on the screen view. If you don't have those extra lines — that is, if you have only the "screen dump" from the ⒫ʳᵗˢᶜʳ⒭ function — you will not know what strategies generated the numbers on the printout.

By the way, if you run into printing difficulty, you can always use Ⓢ to save your analyses, then print the VW.REP file later on.

> **Note:** ValueWar cannot save or print the value view or the graph view. If you try to save or print those views, ValueWar will simply remind you of this limitation; nothing bad will happen.

---

[1] For technical completeness, please note that the printer must be connected to LPT1.
[2] Note the corollary: you can end up with an enormous VW.REP file if you keep appending to it! You can avoid consuming your disk space with that file by using VW.REP (e.g., by printing it or by importing it into another program) and then deleting it when you're done. Use the DOS DEL[ete] command: DEL VW.REP (ENTER).

The graph view

The graph view shows a picture of the current data
You can have ValueWar draw the **graph view** to provide a simple graphic display of the current data in the current period. You can press the (SHIFT)-(F2) key to move immediately to the graph view, or, as described above, you can press (CTRL)-(PGDN) or (CTRL)-(PGUP) repeatedly until you see the graph view. (As described below, the help system will show you which keys work which features.)

- Press (SHIFT)-(F2). A graph will spring onto the screen. It'll show the four competitors' absolute prices for period 0, color-coded as usual.

- Press (↓). The current period advances to period 1, and so does the graph.

- Press (→) three times. The current data and the graph show relative quality.

The other parts of the graph view look and behave exactly like those in the value view. You'll continue to see the data window, the supply/demand window, and the strategy window.

Highlights of the graph view

Here's why you might like ValueWar graphs:

- You can see differences among competitors easily in graphs.

- You might have several people watching ValueWar at one time. It'll be easier for them to see the graph than for them to read the data window.

As described later, you can "animate" the graph just as you can animate the value view. You'll see graphically how any given factor changes during the course of the ValueWar simulation.

The data-history view

The data history shows the entire history of a single factor
ValueWar offers the **data-history view** so that you can see full details of a factor over time. You can display the data history by pressing (SHIFT)-(F3) (or, as usual, by pressing (+) or (-) enough times).

- Press (SHIFT)-(F3) now. ValueWar will switch to the data-history view, displaying whatever factor you were observing in the graph view. (It'll be relative quality, if you've been following along.) The data history shows all four competitors' values on that factor for periods 0 through 20, color-coded as usual. One period will be highlighted; it's the current period.

- Press (↓). The current period changes to period 2. Switching periods doesn't change the data-history view, but if you switch to a view that displays just one period at a time, then that view will use the new period you've selected.

- Press (←)(←)(←). The current data switches to absolute quality, then relative price, and then absolute price; you see all 20 periods, plus the initial position, for each competitor. The data-history view reacts the same way to the (←) and (→) keys as the value view and the graph view.

As described below, you can print or save the analysis shown in the data-history view.

Highlights of the data-history view

The data-history view makes it easy for you to spot trends in competitors' actions or performance. You will find it invaluable if, for example, you want to check for sudden changes in performance, or if you want to see if it takes a long time for a strategy to pay off. You'll also find it useful as a compact summary that compares competitors' performance over the whole simulation.

The competition view

Use the competition view to focus on competitive position

The data-history view shows a single factor at all points in time covered by ValueWar; the **competition view** shows all competitor factors at a single point in time. You can call up the competition view by pressing (SHIFT)-(F4) (or with the ubiquitous (•) or (−)).

- Please press (SHIFT)-(F4). ValueWar will switch to the competition view, with information about each competitor's market position. The current period will remain unchanged from the previous view, but the current data will change if the data from the previous view isn't found in the competition view.

- Press (↓). The current data changes to the next one down, which will be relative price if you've been following the *Tutorial* exactly.

- Press (→). The current period switches to the next one, which is now period 3 if you've been following along. The competition view treats the (←) and (→) keys differently from the data-history view: the competition view uses those keys to switch from one period to another, whereas the data-history view uses them to switch from one factor to another. The general rule to remember with ValueWar is that the (↑) and (↓) keys always move the highlighted row up and down, and since up and down switches from one factor to another in the competition view, ValueWar uses the (←) and (→) keys to move from period to period.

As described below, you can print or save the analysis shown in the competition view.

Highlights of the competition view

The competition view emphasizes competitive differences among the competitors. It helps you assess the competitors' market positions: it helps you see the customer's perspective on the competitors.

The financial-snapshot view

The financial snapshot shows all financial data at one point in time

ValueWar's **financial-snapshot view** is the flip side of the data-history view. Rather than showing all periods for a single factor, the financial snapshot shows all financial factors for a single period.

You can display the financial snapshot by pressing (SHIFT)-(F5) (or via (+) or (-)).

- Press (SHIFT)-(F5) now. You'll see the financial-snapshot view, displaying whatever period you were observing in the data history (period 3 if you've been following along). The data history shows all four competitors' values on financial factors for period 3. The highlighted factor is the current data, which will be absolute price if you've followed the *Tutorial* exactly.

- Press (↓). The current data changes to the next one down in the list, which is sales. Switching data doesn't change the snapshot, but if you switch to a view that displays just one factor at a time, then that view will use the new factor you selected (provided that that factor is available in the new view).

- Press (→). The current period switches to period 4, and you see financial factors for each competitor in that period.

As described below, you can print or save the analysis shown in the financial-snapshot view.

Highlights of the financial-snapshot view

The financial snapshot helps you see the big picture. Through it you can see the financial status of each competitor at one time. Together with the competition view, the financial-snapshot view will help you role-play various competitors by helping you see the totality of their situations.

The profit-and-loss view

The profit-and-loss view summarizes financial results

Strictly speaking, the **profit-and-loss view** is a subset of the financial-snapshot view. It differs in that it is formatted in the style of financial statements.

The profit-and-loss view details the derivation of profits for each competitor. It starts with unit sales and price, subtracts fixed and variable costs, and ends up with profits.
You can display profit and loss by pressing (SHIFT)-(F6) (or (+) or (-)).

- Press (SHIFT)-(F6). You will see the profit-and-loss view right away, with financial results for all four competitors' values in the current period. If you've been pressing keys exactly as described here, you will note that ValueWar is highlighting sales, which is present in both the financial-snapshot and profit-and-loss views.

- Press (↓). The current data changes to the next one down.

- Press (→). The current period switches to the next one, which is period 5 if you've been following along. The profit-and-loss view reacts the same way to the (←) and (→) keys as do the competition and financial-snapshot views.

As described below, you can print or save analysis shown in the profit-and-loss view.

Highlights of the profit-and-loss view

The profit-and-loss view emphasizes financial differences among the competitors. With it you can more easily see whether a competitor is more profitable than the others because it has higher prices or lower costs, or whether another competitor is suffering because its fixed costs are much higher than the other businesses.

The scenario-test view

The scenario test shows how your market strategies perform with different operations strategies or in different environments

You can display the **scenario-test view** after you run the scenario sensitivity test, as described in Chapter 4. Chapter 4 will also describe how to use and interpret the scenario test.

If you have not run the scenario test, and if you nevertheless ask ValueWar to display the scenario-test view with (SHIFT)-(F7) or by pressing (+) or (-) enough times, then ValueWar will inform you that you cannot use that view because you have not performed the necessary calculations. Nothing bad will happen.

Once you have told ValueWar to run the test, you will find that the scenario-test view works very much like the other views. The arrow keys ((←), (→), etc.) switch periods and data, and you can print or save the analysis shown on the screen.

As described later, you can tell ValueWar to simulate the effects of new strategy combinations or of non-strategy moves. If you use either of those features after you've run a scenario test, the results of the test will no longer be up to date. Therefore, the scenario-test view will become unavailable again until you re-run the test. (ValueWar doesn't automatically re-run the test because the test can be time-consuming.)

Highlights of the scenario-test view

The scenario test shows if a strategy works only under special conditions

The scenario-test view offers a very powerful kind of analysis: it tells you whether the effects of the market strategies you've chosen will change if you change your assumptions about operations or the environment ... that is, if you change the scenario.

This analysis is powerful enough to merit a section of its own in Chapter 4. Please refer to that section for more details about the scenario-test view.

The strategy-test view

The strategy test helps you see if you or a competitor should try a new market strategy

You can display the **strategy-test view** after you run the strategy sensitivity test, as described in Chapter 4. Chapter 4 also describes how to use and interpret the test.

If you have not run the strategy test, and if you nevertheless ask ValueWar to display the strategy-test view with (SHIFT)-(F8) or by pressing (+) or (-) enough times, then ValueWar will inform you that you cannot use that view because you have not performed the necessary calculations. Nothing bad will happen.

Once you have told ValueWar to run the test, you will find that the strategy-test view works very much like the other views. The arrow keys ((←), (→), etc.) switch periods and data, and you can print or save the analysis shown on the screen.

As described later, you can tell ValueWar to simulate the effects of new strategy combinations or of non-strategy moves. If you use either of those features after you've run a strategy test, the results of the test will no longer be up to date. Therefore, the strategy-test view will become unavailable again until you re-run the test. (ValueWar doesn't automatically re-run the test because the test can be time-consuming.)

Highlights of the strategy-test view

The strategy test is one of ValueWar's most powerful features

The strategy-test view offers an exceptionally powerful kind of analysis: it shows you how changing the market strategy for one competitor can affect that competitor's, and all the other competitors', performance. Like the scenario test, this analysis is so powerful that it gets a section of its own in Chapter 4. Please refer to that section for more details about the strategy-test view.

Reports

ValueWar can package all its calculations into a compact report that you can peruse on your computer screen or print for documentation, analysis, or reference. You can have ValueWar produce a report by pressing (F9).

Please press (F9). ValueWar will take a few seconds to compose the report, as it tells you in a message box. When it's done, it'll present the top of the report on your screen.

You can do three things with the report.

- Read it on the screen. Use the (↑), (↓), (HOME), (END), (PGUP), and (PGDN) keys to scroll through the report. The report contains all data for every period for every competitor, full supply/demand figures, and a list of the strategies and non-strategy moves taken by each competitor. Information in the report matches what you see in the data, supply/demand, and strategy windows.

- Save it in a disk file that you can print later. To save the report, press Ⓢ while the report is on the screen. ValueWar will save the report in a file named **VW.REP**. If you already have such a file, ValueWar will append its new report to that file; it won't erase what you have already saved.

- Print it, if you have a printer connected to your computer. (Technical note: the printer must be connected to LPT1.) To print the report, press Ⓟ while the report is on the screen. You can interrupt the printing by pressing any key, as ValueWar reminds you with a message on the bottom of the screen. If ValueWar has any trouble printing the report, it will tell you what ails it and ask you to fix the problem. You can resume printing after fixing the problem.

Note: the procedures that you use to save or print the ValueWar report are exactly the same as the procedures you use to save or print ValueWar views, as described above.

You can "import" VW.REP into a word processor or some other program. Tell the importing program that VW.REP is a DOS text file (or, in equivalent technobabble, that VW.REP is a "plain ASCII" or "plain text" file).

You will probably find ValueWar reports invaluable for strategy analysis because they compile all ValueWar data into a compact document. They serve as handy references too, because they contain enough information to recreate your ValueWar simulations.

When you're done with the report, do as the bottom of the screen says: press ⒺⓈⒸ to remove the report from the screen.

The "animate" feature

Use animation to watch the market evolve

You saw in Chapter 2 that you could use "arrow" keys to move the screen from period to period. ValueWar also provides animation to help you watch the market evolve.

Animation works in the value view and in the graph view; it's the most fun in the former. Please press ⓈⒽⒾⒻⓉ-Ⓕ1 to make sure the value view is on the screen.

When you have the value view or the graph view on the screen, please press Ⓕ10. ValueWar will immediately move to period 0. Then it'll advance period by period through all 20 subsequent periods, at a rate of about 1 period per second. You can watch the competitors jockey for position as years of infighting unfold.

If you want to interrupt the animation, just press any key. ValueWar will halt the show.

ValueWar provides two variations on the animation theme. One: you can animate from the current period up to the last period. Press ⓉⒶⒷ to do so. Two: you can animate from period 0 up to the current period. Hold either ⓈⒽⒾⒻⓉ key down, then press ⓉⒶⒷ. You can interrupt these variations just as you could interrupt the Ⓕ10 version.

More about the help system

You saw in Chapter 2 how you could use the (F2) key to get a definition for a scenario, strategy, or data. We alluded mysteriously to additional help features. Here they are.

Use (F1) for ValueWar's help system You enter the ValueWar help system via the (F1) key at any point in the program. The help you get will depend on what's happening at the time you press (F1); in other words, you get "context sensitive" help.

```
What kind of help would you like?

a: VW commands and keys

b: Analyses and options

c: How to read the screen

d: Scenario information

e: Printing and saving

f: About "views"

g: Miscellaneous items

h: About ValueWar
```

ValueWar's help menu

Press (F1) now, please. You should see the **help menu**, a menu with eight options, in the middle of the screen. We'll discuss each of the items in that menu.

Note also that the bottom line of the screen says that you can get help with the (F1) key. Yes, you can get help about help: (F1) gets you a brief description of the help system. You can also get a definition of each item in the help menu with (F2), just as you can get definitions of items in other menus.

Here are the eight kinds of help you can get:

- *VW commands and keys*. If you select this kind of help, you'll see a list of keys that ValueWar recognizes at the point you've reached in the program.

- *Analyses and options*. This kind of help tells you more about the options that you can invoke (as opposed to the keys you press to invoke them).

- *How to read the screen*. Select this kind of help to refresh your memory about the current screen (i.e., the screen that's underneath the help menu).

- *Scenario information*. Selecting this option will pop up the first of a series of windows that describe in detail the scenario you're simulating with ValueWar (see below for more information). If you're in the scenario menu, you'll find this capability helpful for figuring out which scenario to choose.

- *Printing and saving*. This help message will tell you how you print or save ValueWar views and reports. It reprises the information presented above on the subjects of printing and saving.

- *About 'views'*. Select this option if you want a list of ValueWar's views and of the keys you can press to access them. This list also duplicates information presented earlier in the *Tutorial*.

- *Miscellaneous items*. This kind of help lets you know about ValueWar capabilities that don't fit neatly into the other categories. Version 1.64 of ValueWar has one such item: if you hold down the (ALT) key and press (C). ValueWar will pop up a window that will help you adjust the color controls on your monitor.

- *About ValueWar.* You will see a brief message about ValueWar's objectives and how you can contact its authors.

You can select the kind of help you want with the techniques you use with all other ValueWar menus. One: type the first letter of the menu for the kind of help you want (for example, type (f) for help about views). Two: use the arrow keys to move the highlight to the kind of help you want, then press (ENTER).

ValueWar's help system is fairly elaborate, but it takes just a keystroke or two to get almost any information about your ValueWar simulations. We recommend that you browse through the help system frequently so that ValueWar can remind you about all the options at your disposal.

Scenario-information help

The ValueWar help system is particularly useful when it comes to understanding ValueWar scenarios and how ValueWar works in general.

ValueWar takes about seventy factors into account in its simulations. These factors range from market growth to the time it takes for customers to realize that competitors have made changes in the quality and/or price of their products and services. These factors comprise ValueWar scenarios, and it is with the scenario-information help that you can see those factors for your ValueWar scenarios. Scenarios embody operations strategies for your business and its competitors, as well as market and customer data.

Scenario information appears in several windows The scenario information appears in a series of windows, each of which contains several factors. The first time you request scenario-information help, you will see the first of those windows, from which you can switch to the others; on subsequent requests, ValueWar will automatically return you to the window you last viewed.

Once you've called up any scenario-information window, you can see the additional windows by using the (←) and (→) keys. If you have multiple scenarios, you can see scenario information on each scenario by pressing the (PGUP) and (PGDN) keys.

You can get definitions of scenario factors You can also get definitions of individual factors by pressing the (F2) key. ValueWar will pop up one of its definition windows. (For yet more detail, consult the *Reference* section of this book.) You "point" to factors by pressing the (↑) and (↓) keys until ValueWar has highlighted the factor you want to define.

You don't have to remember which keys do what. As the bottom line of the screen says, you can always press (F1) while you're perusing the scenario-information windows, and ValueWar will remind you which keys have which effects.

Summary

In this chapter of the *Tutorial* you've explored ValueWar's views, reports, animation, and help. You now know most of what ValueWar can do, and you know how to use the help system to get more information when you need it.

In Chapter 4 you'll see ValueWar's powerful "what-if" features that let you switch scenarios, switch strategies, and override strategies. You'll also see ValueWar's sensitivity tests.

Advanced ValueWar

This chapter introduces you to more-advanced ValueWar techniques.

If you're running the ValueWar demo while you're going through the *Tutorial*, please set up the software so that you're where you'd be if you just finished Chapter 2:

Scenario	Horse race
View....................................	Value view
Amalgamated.....................	Highest Q and P
BigBiz.................................	Highest Q, steady P
Consolidated	Lowest Q and P
Diversified	Follow success
Current data......................	Absolute price
Current period	0 (initial position)

In this chapter we'll show how to switch scenarios and strategies and how to implement "non-strategy" moves. We'll end the chapter with ValueWar's two sensitivity analyses.

Switching scenarios

You recall that the first thing you did with ValueWar was to select a scenario for your simulations ("Horse race," in this case). ValueWar lets you switch to a different scenario at will. This capability lets you see how the strategies you select perform under different circumstances.

In a version of ValueWar calibrated for a particular business, the scenarios will represent alternative futures for that business[1]. In the ValueWar demo, the scenarios represent different variations on the Horse-race theme, which means that you can see whether strategies that are sensible for one scenario — that is, strategies that work under one set of assumptions about the market and competitors — may lead to disaster under another. The scenario-sensitivity test, discussed a little later, offers another way to examine your strategies under different scenarios.

---

[1] For example, most-likely growth, best-case growth, and worst-case growth, or price-sensitive versus quality-sensitive customers. By manipulating scenarios with the ValueWar Calibrator software you can simulate a very wide variety of different market, competitive, and cost conditions.

In this section of the *Tutorial* we'll discuss how to switch scenarios, but we won't actually make the switch. But feel free to experiment; nothing bad will happen.

**Use (F3)
to switch
scenarios**

Here's how to switch scenarios:

- Any view may be on the screen except for the scenario-test view or the strategy-test view. (If either of those views is on the screen, ValueWar will automatically switch to a view from which it can switch scenarios.)

- Press (F3) to call up the scenarios menu. (ValueWar can't switch scenarios from all views, so the view may change automatically.)

- Use the arrow keys to move the highlight to the scenario you want to select.

- If you wanted to select the highlighted scenario, you'd press (ENTER). For now, please press (ESC) to tell ValueWar not to switch scenarios.

You can use (F1) (help) and (F2) (definitions) to get information about the scenario highlighted on the menu, just as you could the first time you saw the scenarios menu.

If you were to select a new scenario, ValueWar would recalculate all its data and replace the current information on the screen with the new data. However, because you've retained the current scenario by backing-up from the scenarios menu, ValueWar simply removes the menu and behaves as though nothing happened (which, from its perspective, is exactly what happened).

**Market strat-
egies don't
change when
you change
scenarios**

Important: When you select a new scenario, ValueWar retains all the market-strategy decisions you made. *Switching scenarios makes ValueWar simulate the effect of those strategies under new conditions.* With appropriate scenarios calibrated and installed, you can analyze key uncertainties facing a business. See the *Reference* section of this book for more information about scenarios.

It doesn't matter which period is the current period when you switch scenarios. ValueWar recalculates everything from period 0 to period 20 with the new scenario.

Switching market strategies

Switching market strategies in ValueWar resembles switching scenarios: you call up the strategy menu and point to the ones you want each competitor to use, or you press (ESC) to cancel your request. (To switch operations strategies, you'd alter factors with the ValueWar Calibrator software.)

New market strategies take effect at the current period!

> **Important:** When you select one or more new market strategies, *ValueWar recalculates data starting from the current period, not from period 0.* This system lets you simulate mid-course changes in strategies. Thus, if the current period is number 10, and if you select new strategies for one or more businesses, then you'll simulate the old strategies for periods 1 through 9 and the new strategies for periods 10 through 20.
>
> This calculation process is different from switching scenarios. When you switch scenarios, ValueWar recalculates all periods (with the same strategies you already had); when you switch strategies, ValueWar keeps the same scenario and recalculates just the periods from which you initiated the new strategies.

Use (F4) to change market strategies

Let's change Diversified's strategy, imagining that its management wants to emulate its largest competitor, not its most profitable competitor.

- First, please press (HOME) to set the current period to 0. Doing so means that you'll have ValueWar change Diversified's strategy for the entire simulation.

- Press (F4) to start the strategy menus. Notice that ValueWar switched the current period to 1 from 0. It made the switch because you can't have a strategy in period 0. (ValueWar can't set new strategies from all views, so the view might change automatically.)

- ValueWar puts up a strategy menu for Amalgamated first. Note that the highlight is already on Amalgamated's current strategy. We're not going to change Amalgamated's strategy, so press (ENTER) to retain — actually, to re-select — its old strategy.

- ValueWar shows the strategy menu in succession for BigBiz and Consolidated. Since we're not changing their strategies either, please press (ENTER) twice.[1]

- You should now see the strategy menu for Diversified, with "Follow success" highlighted. Select "Match #1's Q and P" instead, either by pressing (↑) three times and then (ENTER), or by typing (K).

ValueWar discerns that you have indeed selected one or more new strategies, so it recalculates the simulation. It will recalculate all the periods because you selected new strategies to take effect from period 1.

When it's finished calculating, you'll see the value view again. But it'll look different: the strategy window will display a new strategy for Diversified, and the data window will show new data.

---

[1] Incidentally, you can back up to a previous competitor by pressing the (ESC) key. If you press (ESC) enough times, you'll remove the strategy menus and no changes will occur. If you keep pressing (ESC), you'll eventually quit running ValueWar altogether.

> **Note:** although you may not change the *strategies* for some businesses, their *actions* may nonetheless change dramatically. For example, in this case Amalgamated's actions will change *because of* Diversified's new strategy. Diversified's old strategy, "Follow success," made Diversified follow Amalgamated's price increases, which made Amalgamated continue to raise its price (since its strategy was "Highest Q and P"). But when Diversified switched to "Match #1's Q and P," it emulated someone other than Amalgamated, and so Amalgamated was satisfied with a more-modest price increase.

Non-strategy moves

You may want to override a market strategy: perhaps it causes a business to hold its price steady, and you'd like to see if the business could get away with a one-time price cut instead. Another strategy might stifle the quality improvements that a business seems to need, and you'd like to see if improving its quality would pay off.

Non-strategy moves let you override strategies. Use (F7)*.*

ValueWar lets you select quality and price moves for any business in any period by using an option called **non-strategy moves** (**NSM**s).

NSMs let you override business strategies for a single period at a time. If you wish, you can even use NSMs for all 20 periods. The business strategies you selected operate normally for the periods in which you do not make NSMs.

- Please press (PGDN). If you've been following along with the *Tutorial*, the current period should be 5. If it isn't, please press the ⊕ or ⊕ key to move to period 5.

- Now press (F7) to start the NSM process. A miniature value map will pop up in the middle of the screen, with a yellow box for Amalgamated in its center. The box will say "Q=,P=," a shorthand expression for "hold quality, hold price." The longhand version will appear just below the chart. (ValueWar can't use NSMs in all views, so the view might change automatically.)

- Press ⊕. Notice that the box moved up, the box says "Q=,P^," and the explanation below says "hold quality, raise price."

- Try pressing the other "arrow" keys (⊕, ⊕, ⊕, (HOME), (END), (PGUP), (PGDN)). Notice that the box moves to the position indicated by the key's position on the keyboard's numeric keypad. Notice also that the way you move the box corresponds to the direction the NSM would take on the value map. In other words, you're pointing the box toward your NSM's goal for the business on the value map in the value view. It's as though you were taking hold of a business on the value map and shoving it in a particular direction.

- Please press (PGUP). The yellow box should be in the upper right corner, and it should say "Q^,P^" to indicate an increase in both quality and price. Press (ENTER) to select that NSM.

- Now you should see the original NSM window, but with a cyan box for BigBiz instead.[1] Please move the box by pressing (PGDN) (you could also press (↓) and then (→)). The window should say "Q^,Pv." Press (ENTER) to accept that NSM.

Use (INS) to
***not* override a**
business's
strategy

- Suppose you want Consolidated and Diversified to continue to use their strategies, not a NSM. You can say so by using the (INS) key, which tells ValueWar that you don't want to override that business's market strategy. Please press (INS) twice, once for Consolidated, once for Diversified.

The NSM window vanishes, and ValueWar recalculates its data with the new moves. It recalculates starting with period 5; nothing has changed for periods 0 through 4.

When it's done, you'll notice new entries in the strategy window for Amalgamated and BigBiz, and you'll see modest changes in their data. We'll discuss the effects of the NSMs in greater length in Chapter 5.

ValueWar enforces various constraints, calibrated for specific business situations, upon competitors' ranges of action. (You can observe those constraints; they're part of the scenario information accessible via the help system. See also the *Reference* section of this book.) If a competitor has already raised its quality as much as it can, for example, its NSM window will refuse to accept a move that would cause it to improve quality still further. The NSM window will let you know when constraints are in effect for a competitor.

Scenario-sensitivity analysis

ValueWar's two **sensitivity analyses** help you determine whether any businesses would act differently or perform differently under different circumstances. One of the sensitivity analyses tests the sensitivity of the businesses to the scenario (which includes the effects of operations strategies); the other tests the sensitivity of a single business to its choice of market strategy. We'll discuss the scenario-test analysis first.

The scenario
test checks
strategies in
different
environments

The **scenario-test** analysis explores the degree to which the actions or performance of the four businesses would change if the scenario were to change. In other words, it helps you see how the businesses' performance depends on your choice of scenario … that is, to your assumptions about the future.

ValueWar performs its scenario test by taking the market strategies and NSMs you've chosen and running those strategies and NSMs for *every* scenario, not just the one displayed on the screen. It then presents a summary in which you can see the extent to which the scenario affects the businesses' results.

---

[1] If you were to press (ESC), you would return to Amalgamated, and if you were to press (ESC) yet again, you'd cancel the NSM process.

Use (F5) for the scenario test
Here's how to run the scenario test: press the (F5) key. That's it. Please press (F5) now. ValueWar will run its calculations, keeping you informed of its progress. (ValueWar can't run the scenario test from all views, so it might change the view automatically.)

Scenario tests take a relatively long time to run because they simulate your chosen strategies with all the scenarios, not just one. How much time? On a 486-class computer, perhaps 2 seconds. On a PC- or XT-class computer without an 8087 math co-processor chip, more like several minutes. As it says on the bottom of the screen, you can interrupt ValueWar's calculations if you decide you don't want to wait.

By the way, ValueWar tries to save you time. For example, it doesn't recalculate the current scenario as it simulates each scenario for the scenario test. In addition, it remembers the results of the scenario test so that they're immediately accessible — that is, they don't have to be recalculated — the next time you ask for them. They stay accessible until you change strategies or NSMs, which render invalid the prior tests.[1]

When ValueWar has completed the scenario test, it automatically switches to the **scenario-test view**. The scenario-test view contains a complete summary of a single factor for a single period, for all competitors under all scenarios. If you've been following along with the *Tutorial*, you should see "Absolute price" at the top of the window, with "Period 5 (Y2/Q1)" right below.

The (←), (→), (↑), (↓), (HOME), (END), etc., keys work exactly as they do in other views. They change the data and the period for which the scenario test is shown.

Under the left column in the scenario-test view, you'll see a list of all the scenarios. One of them, the current scenario, will be identified with a "■." That's the scenario you were using in your analysis prior to requesting the scenario test.

The next four columns show the data for each of the four businesses, color-coded as usual. The numbers you see in the Horse-race row (your current scenario) match the numbers you see in the data window on the value view. The numbers in the other rows correspond to what you would see in the data window if you were to change the current scenario.

The last column, "Average," shows the average of the numbers in each row.

Underneath the list of scenarios you'll find two more rows:

- The **average** row is the simple average of the column above. Unless you've changed the current data, you'll see the average absolute price that each business charged in the various scenarios.

---

[1] The scenario test may also have to be recalculated if your PC has a small amount of memory available to ValueWar and if you run another memory-intensive analysis, such as the strategy-sensitivity test, after you run the scenario test. ValueWar recycles memory as needed so that it can perform the analyses you request.

- The **standard deviation** row shows the standard deviation of the numbers in the column above. It measures the variability in the current data for each business, which shows the business's sensitivity to the choice of scenario.

If a business's standard deviation is relatively high,[1] the business is more sensitive to the choice of scenario than are its competitors. In other words, its data vary more, across scenarios, than do its competitors'.

> **Warning:** The formula for calculating standard deviations may cause the size of the businesses to affect the relative sizes of their standard deviations. A business with relatively high sales will often have higher standard deviations on other size-dependent data, such as fixed costs, unit capacity, and so on.

ValueWar is normally calibrated with scenarios expressing variations on a common theme, such as different assumptions about customer preferences or market growth; they're comparable because the scenarios start with the same competitors in the same positions. You could look at the standard deviations to see, for example, which businesses' profits are most sensitive to your scenario assumptions.

In the ValueWar demo, you can see that a given set of market strategies can produce different results under different environments. For example, if you have pressed the keys suggested by the *Tutorial*, and if you now press (END) (to move to period 20) and (←) or (→) (to display data on profits), you would see that the current set of strategies generally yields profits for all the competitors, with the dramatic exception of the "Seasonal horse race" and "Recession horse race" scenarios, in which Consolidated in particular performs much worse *with its chosen strategies* than it does under other scenarios. Diversified shows the greatest variability in results, as evidenced by the standard-deviation row. So, we have discovered that the performance of the current set of strategies is indeed sensitive to assumptions about the market. We could conclude that some strategies are not appropriate for a seasonal or recession market. So, if we think that the market might be seasonal or enter a recession, the competitors should search for different strategies.

As with reports and other views, you can read the scenario test on the screen, save it in a file for later use, or print it. Refer to the instructions in Chapter 3, or call up the "Printing and saving" help from the help system.

When you're done looking at the scenario-test view, you can switch to another view with the techniques you've seen already. And now that you've calculated the scenario test, you can quickly recall the scenario-test view with (SHIFT)-(F7) or by looping with the (+) or (-) keys. You'll

---

[1] You cannot say whether a given standard deviation is "high" or "low". All you can do is compare standard deviations to see which businesses seem more or less sensitive.

get fast response because, your PC's memory permitting, ValueWar doesn't recalculate the test until you change strategies or NSMs, so it can re-display the scenario-test view without delay.

Strategy-sensitivity analysis

Would a different strategy make a difference? ValueWar's second sensitivity analysis, the **strategy test**, explores a business's sensitivity to its choice of market strategy. In other words, it checks the business's performance for every strategy in the strategy menu so that you can see if another strategy would do better (or worse) than its current strategy. It also shows how much the *other* businesses would be affected by each strategy that the chosen business could follow.

ValueWar performs the strategy test by running every strategy for a business you select, while holding constant the strategies followed by the other businesses. It runs those strategies from the current period on.[1] Thus, if the current period were period 6, then the strategy test will test the effects of different strategies for the chosen business from periods 6 through 20. The strategies you selected for periods 1–5 remain unchanged.

> **Note:** Since they contain information about cost structures, capabilities for changing quality and price, speed of reaction, and so on, scenarios express operations strategies as well as assumptions about the market. Therefore, the scenario test can explore the effects of different operations strategies just as the strategy test explores the effects of different market strategies.

Actions may change even if strategies don't

> **Note:** Although the *strategies* remain unchanged for the businesses other than the one whose market strategy you're testing, their *actions* may change dramatically. For example, say you're testing the strategy for a competitor that's the clear market leader and that all the other businesses follow the "Match #1's Q and P" strategy. When ValueWar tests the "Highest Q and P" strategy for the leader, the other businesses will try to match its *rising* quality and price; when ValueWar tests the "Lowest Q and P" strategy for the leader, the other businesses will try to match its *falling* quality and price.

Move to period 6 with the ⊕ or ⊕ keys to start the strategy test in the period right after the NSMs you specified. The strategy-test analysis requires two keystrokes:

---

[1] Note that this procedure means that ValueWar overrides all strategy changes and NSMs for the competitor whose strategy you're testing; other competitors' strategies remain unchanged.

Use F6 for the strategy test

- Press F6 to start the strategy test. ValueWar will display a menu asking you to select a business on which to perform the test. (ValueWar can't run the strategy test from all views, so it may change the view automatically.)

- Press the letter next to the business whose strategy you want to test, or highlight the desired business with the arrow keys and press ENTER.

Please press F6 now, then press A to test strategies for Amalgamated. As with the scenario test, ValueWar will start calculating, keeping you informed of its progress, and letting you stop its work by pressing any key.

ValueWar will remember the results of the strategy test so that it can immediately access the test if you want to see it again. ValueWar will only recalculate the test if you change the period from which you're requesting the test, if you change the business whose strategy you wish to test, if you change the scenario, if you change any business's strategy, or if it had to recycle memory to run a subsequent analysis.

When its calculations are complete, ValueWar puts the **strategy-test view** on the screen. This view looks and behaves just like the scenario-test view, with these exceptions:

- Instead of a list of scenarios, you'll see a list of strategies. The list matches the strategies in the strategy menu because ValueWar has run every strategy for the business you chose.

- One of the business columns will be highlighted at the top with special characters to indicate that the tests apply to that business (for example, . A , indicates that we tested Competitor A's strategies). In other words, the different strategies were tested for that business, while all the other businesses kept their existing strategies.

- As usual, you can use the ← and → keys to view all the data, and you can use the ↑, ↓, HOME, END, PGUP, and PGDN keys to change to other periods. However, you cannot switch to a period prior to the one at which you began the strategy test.

Please press the END key to move to period 20, then press the ← or → keys until the data for "Cumulative profits" is displayed in the strategy-test view.[1] If you've faithfully followed the *Tutorial* so far, you'll see these numbers:

---

[1] You can tell ValueWar to automatically move to period 20 at the end of every strategy test you run. Use the /LAST switch when you start up ValueWar. You'd type VW /LAST.

```
Strategy test          Cumulative profits
(Periods 6 - 20)       Period 20 (Y5/Q4)

Strategy for A     ►   A   ◄     B         C         D        Average

Don't change Q or P    67,314    56,209    43,031    55,200    55,439
Highest Q and P        69,606    53,220    42,586    52,228    54,410
Highest Q, steady P    69,606    53,220    42,586    52,228    54,410
Steady Q, lowest P     46,192    51,165    33,484    51,389    45,558
Raise Q and P          69,683    53,237    42,608    52,244    54,443
Raise Q, lag P         69,606    53,220    42,586    52,228    54,410
Lowest Q and P         43,569    58,902    31,539    58,543    48,138
P by supply/demand     67,314    56,209    43,031    55,200    55,439
Highest Q, average P   52,075    53,416    38,580    48,897    48,242
Match mkt average      54,228    51,796    39,951    51,487    49,366
Match #1's Q and P     56,544    54,200    41,886    52,328    51,239
Beat #1's price        44,966    51,734    33,205    47,364    44,317
Lead Q and P up        69,683    53,237    42,608    52,244    54,443
Follow success         67,314    56,209    43,031    55,200    55,439
Tit for best tat       67,314    56,209    43,031    55,200    55,439

Average                61,001    54,146    40,250    52,799
Standard deviation     10,205     2,149     4,099     2,756
```

Note that the view reminds you that you ran the strategy-test analysis for 15 periods of the simulation, as indicated by the "(Periods 6 – 20)" comment in the upper left corner.

According to the upper right corner, you're currently viewing cumulative profits for period 20. Also, because the column for Amalgamated (Competitor A) is emphasized, you know that ValueWar has tested all strategies for Amalgamated while holding constant the strategies you already chose for the other three competitors.

Here's what we can conclude from this snippet of analysis:

- We chose the "Highest Q and P" strategy for Amalgamated prior to running the strategy test. The cumulative profits generated by that strategy, which are 69,606 in period 20, are quite high; no other strategy performs even one percent better, and several strategies perform much worse.

- The "Beat #1's price" strategy apparently starts a war that devastates all the businesses. Looking at the strategy test, Amalgamated would learn that this strategy is not just aggressive; it's self-destructive.

- No strategy *for Amalgamated* provides better performance for Amalgamated *and* its competitors. Amalgamated's competitors can do better, if Amalgamated finds it prudent to sacrifice some of its profits for peace.

- Several strategies yield identical results. However, *Amalgamated should not conclude that those strategies are identical*; they produce identical results only because of the strategies that its competitors have chosen[1]. Selecting different strategies for its competitors might change the results from those seemingly identical strategies.

- Consolidated's results vary more than BigBiz's or Diversified's, meaning that if Consolidated sticks with its strategy, it is more sensitive to Amalgamated's choice of strategy. Moreover, its cumulative profits are always the worst of the four.

As with reports and other views, you can read the strategy test on the screen, save it in a file for later use, or print it. Refer to the instructions in Chapter 3, or call up the "Printing and saving" help from the help system.

When you're done looking at the strategy-test view, you can switch to another view with the techniques you've seen already. ValueWar will revert to the strategies and NSMs that were in effect prior to the strategy test. You can review the strategy test very easily, though: now that you've calculated the strategy test, you can call up the strategy-test view with (SHIFT)-(F7) or by looping with the (•) or (-) keys.

Summary

In Chapter 4 you've seen how to switch scenarios, how to switch strategies for competitors, and how to override strategies via non-strategy moves. These techniques are central to analysis with ValueWar because they let you simulate what would happen to each competitor under different market conditions (i.e., scenarios) and with different competitive reactions (i.e., strategies and NSMs).

You've also seen ValueWar's two sensitivity analyses, which provide a quick way to test the effect that scenarios or strategies — that is, your assumptions about the environment and about the choice of strategies — have on the actions that businesses take and on the performance that results.

You've seen all of ValueWar's features. We suggest that you spend some time trying different strategies for each competitor. You might find it helpful to ask yourself questions such as:

- How long would a competitor wait to have its performance improve?
- Would a business switch strategy if it saw its competitors getting better results?
- Can a business dig itself into a hole from which it can't emerge?
- Can businesses with different strategies perform equally well?
- Is it better to go head-to-head with a competitor or to find separate niches?

---

[1] For example, "Highest Q and P" and "Highest Q, steady P" produced the same results when tested for periods 6-20. That's because by period 6 Amalgamated had already achieved the highest price, and so it didn't have to raise its price any more ... thereby executing the same actions as would holding its priced steady. If, however, a competitor had raised its prices, then Amalgamated would react (and perform) differently under the two strategies.

- Can one business cause its three competitors to perform badly?

Chapter 5 will discuss in detail the results that ensue from the simulation you ran through the *Tutorial*. Chapter 6 will explore additional ValueWar simulations to make the strategy analysis more complete. The *Reference* section will help you understand ValueWar's behavior and how calibrating ValueWar's factors can make ValueWar simulate your own markets.

ValueWar In Depth

This chapter will interpret the report you'd get from following the *Tutorial's* instructions through Chapter 4 and then pressing (F9). It presents the report, page by page, complete with commentary on ValueWar's calculations and their implications for business strategy.

> **Important:** Do not apply this report to your own business situation! Different environments (scenarios) lead to different results, so ValueWar must be calibrated for specific businesses. (See the *Reference* section of this book.) And different strategies can yield *very* different results, as you'll see in Chapter 6.

Description of simulation

```
ValueWar(TM) Version 1.64.  Run at 9:22 a.m., Monday, August 30, 1993.

Scenario:      Horse race
Competitors:   A: Amalgamated, Inc.
               B: BigBiz Corporation
               C: Consolidated Company
               D: Diversified Limited

Market strategies and non-strategy moves (NSMs):
 a: Don't change Q or P    f: Raise Q, lag P      k: Match #1's Q and P
 b: Highest Q and P        g: Lowest Q and P      l: Beat #1's price
 c: Highest Q, steady P    h: P by supply/demand  m: Lead Q and P up
 d: Steady Q, lowest P     i: Highest Q, average P n: Follow success
 e: Raise Q and P          j: Match mkt average   o: Tit for best tat

nsm1: Cut Q, cut P      nsm4: Cut Q, hold P      nsm7: Cut Q, raise P
nsm2: Hold Q, cut P     nsm5: Hold Q, hold P     nsm8: Hold Q, raise P
nsm3: Raise Q, cut P    nsm6: Raise Q, hold P    nsm9: Raise Q, raise P
```

The report starts by describing the simulation you ran: the name of the scenario, the names of the competitors, and the strategies and NSMs available to them. This information matches the options on the scenario, strategy, and NSM menus.

The ValueWar report uses the codes shown alongside the strategies and NSMs to identify each competitor's action in each period. Thus, "e" refers to the Raise Q and P strategy, and "nsm9" means the Raise Q, raise P non-strategy move.

Strategy history

```
Market-strategy history:
  Per    A      B     C     D
  ---  -----  ----- ----- -----
   1     b      c     g     k
   2     b      c     g     k
   3     b      c     g     k
   4     b      c     g     k

   5    nsm9   nsm3   g     k
   6     b      c     g     k
   7     b      c     g     k
   8     b      c     g     k

   9     b      c     g     k
  10     b      c     g     k
  11     b      c     g     k
  12     b      c     g     k

  13     b      c     g     k
  14     b      c     g     k
  15     b      c     g     k
  16     b      c     g     k

  17     b      c     g     k
  18     b      c     g     k
  19     b      c     g     k
  20     b      c     g     k
```

The first page of the report concludes by listing the strategies that each business used in each period. For example, business D, Diversified, used strategy k, "Match #1's Q and P," for all 20 periods. Competitor A used "Highest Q and P" for all periods except for period 5, in which it used the "Raise Q, raise P" non-strategy move.

This information corresponds to what you saw in the strategy window on the ValueWar screen. The only difference is that the report uses codes (letters or NSM numbers) instead of strategy names; the names are too long to fit across the page.

Market summary

Per	Unit supply	Unit demand	Prcvd avg quality	Prcvd avg price
0	50000	40000	70.0	1.00
1	50000	40688	70.5	1.00
2	50000	41448	71.5	1.01
3	50000	42390	73.0	1.00
4	50237	43330	74.5	1.00
5	51050	44290	76.0	1.00
6	51832	45479	78.1	0.99
7	52471	46610	80.1	0.99
8	53331	47754	82.1	0.99
9	54356	48920	84.2	0.99
10	55676	50109	86.2	0.99
11	58006	51312	88.2	0.99
12	60080	52558	90.3	0.99
13	60705	53693	91.8	0.99
14	61308	54648	92.5	0.99
15	61865	55497	92.6	0.99
16	65853	56302	92.6	0.99
17	66063	57131	92.5	0.99
18	67500	57968	92.5	0.99
19	67500	58811	92.6	0.99
20	67500	59674	92.6	0.99

ValueWar calculates several numbers that summarize events in the market.

The **unit supply** and **unit demand** columns indicate, respectively, the number of units that the four competitors could produce and the number of units that the customers in the market want to buy. The data in these columns correspond to the data in the supply/demand window in the quality/price and graph views.

Unit supply depends on several scenario factors. (You can use ValueWar's help system to get an on-screen description of the scenario, as covered in Chapter 3. See the *Reference* section for details on scenario factors.) For example, businesses can usually add some capacity by debottlenecking, but regular additions take more time. Regular capacity additions take 8 periods — that is, 2 years — in the ValueWar demonstration[1].

Businesses seek to maintain a target level of capacity utilization because increasing capacity increases costs. Hence, businesses won't add regular capacity until they pass their individual utilization targets. They're equally conservative with respect to debottlenecking. However, they

---

[1] You can use the ValueWar Calibrator software (not provided with the demo version of ValueWar) to set factors to value that best match your own business, market, and competitors.

can procrastinate on debottlenecking because they can debottleneck instantaneously, whereas regular additions take more time and therefore generally happen in advance so as to avoid stockouts.[1]

In the demo, it happens that the competitors' total supply never falls short of the market's demand. Nevertheless, they must add capacity after about a year to keep up with growing demand.

The base growth rate for unit demand in the Horse-race scenario is about 6%. However, the market may be incrementally stimulated or depressed by the quality offered and prices charged by the businesses. In this case, average prices decline slightly over five years and average quality rises substantially. Lower prices and higher quality encourage existing customers to buy more and entice new customers to start buying. As a result, unit demand grows somewhat faster than it would have, had businesses left their products unchanged. The extent of the market's demand elasticity depends on factors calibrated for each scenario (see the *Reference* section of this book).

The **perceived average quality** and **perceived average price** columns show the average of the quality offered and the prices charged by the businesses in the market. These numbers appear only in the ValueWar report. They are "perceived" because they reflect the time delay, if any, in customers' perception of quality and price changes. (See the "customer perception time" factor in the *Reference* section.) In other words, these numbers show what customers think are current quality and price, but they may actually show quality and price averages that are out of date.

Note that average price hovers at 1.00 or 1.01 for the first 5 periods, then drops in period 6, and holds still at 0.99 from then on. This pattern usually means that a business made a non-strategy move or changed its strategy, and that its competitors did not react (on average). In this case, though, we'll presently see a different explanation.

Note also that average quality marches steadily up until period 14, whereupon it abruptly stops rising (a blip in periods 17 and 18 is due to rounding). Such a pattern generally indicates that one or more businesses hit a constraint, as set by scenario factors; that is, they were unable to change more, even if they wanted to. It might also signal a change in strategy, but we know from the strategy-history page of the report that no changes occurred around period 14.

---

[1] Capacity triggers are usually set at some point below 100% utilization, which means that the competitor doesn't want to risk stockouts. In some cases, however, the trigger point may be set over 100%, which would prevent the competitor from adding capacity until it became reasonably sure that it could fill that capacity. Such a high trigger could mean that the competitor's capacity is very expensive, suggesting that stockouts hurt less than underutilized capacity, or that customer loyalty is very low, suggesting that temporary stockouts won't cause customers to defect for long periods of time.

Absolute price and relative price

| | Absolute price | | | | Relative price | | | |
Per	A	B	C	D	A	B	C	D
0	1.00	1.00	1.00	1.00	100	100	100	100
1	1.02	1.00	0.98	1.00	102	100	98	100
2	1.04	1.00	0.96	1.02	104	99	96	101
3	1.06	1.00	0.95	1.00	106	100	95	100
4	1.06	1.00	0.95	1.00	106	100	95	100
5	1.08	0.98	0.95	1.00	108	98	95	100
6	1.08	0.98	0.93	0.98	109	99	94	99
7	1.08	0.98	0.93	0.98	109	99	94	99
8	1.08	0.98	0.93	0.98	109	99	94	99
9	1.08	0.98	0.93	0.98	109	99	94	99
10	1.08	0.98	0.93	0.98	109	99	94	99
11	1.08	0.98	0.93	0.98	109	99	94	99
12	1.08	0.98	0.93	0.98	109	99	94	99
13	1.08	0.98	0.93	0.98	109	99	94	99
14	1.08	0.98	0.93	0.98	109	99	94	99
15	1.08	0.98	0.93	0.98	109	99	94	99
16	1.08	0.98	0.93	0.98	109	99	94	99
17	1.08	0.98	0.93	0.98	109	99	94	99
18	1.08	0.98	0.93	0.98	109	99	94	99
19	1.08	0.98	0.93	0.98	109	99	94	99
20	1.08	0.98	0.93	0.98	109	99	94	99

Absolute price means the actual prices charged by each business. **Relative price** shows each business's absolute price divided by the average of all the businesses' prices.

Customers take relative price into account when they decide which competitor's product to buy. However, no business can unilaterally determine its relative price; it can only determine its *absolute* price. Each business's relative price depends not only on its absolute price but also on its competitors' absolute prices. Thus, a business may effectively raise its relative price by taking no action at all while its competitors all cut their prices.

Note: if all businesses raise their absolute prices, their relative prices don't change much.[1] Nonetheless, the overall increase will affect everyone's performance because, as noted earlier, market demand depends partly on the average price charged. In other words, no one suffers a competitive blow if everyone raises prices, but the market will penalize everyone by growing a little less rapidly than if prices had stayed lower.

---

[1] Well, relative prices change a little even if all absolute prices move in concert. A difference of 5 cents per unit translates to 5.0% on relative price if the average price is 1.00, but it's only 4.5% if the average price rises to 1.10.

In the demo, we see Amalgamated and Consolidated immediately change their prices. Amalgamated's strategy is "Highest Q and P," so it bumps its price up to 1.02, 1.04, and 1.06 in periods 1, 2, and 3. Consolidated wants to have the "Lowest Q and P," so it cuts its price to 0.98, 0.96, and 0.95 over the same span.

The rates at which the businesses changed their prices come from the scenario's factors (see the *Reference* section). In this case, prices can go up or down no faster than 2% per period. ValueWar won't allow prices to fall below some percentage of variable costs per unit (the percentage is set by a scenario factor and is generally over 100%).

Consolidated slowed its rate of change in period 3. It did so because it reached a position lower-enough than its competitors'. "Enough" is defined via scenario factors; see the *Reference* section for more details. Amalgamated would have slowed in period 3 if it weren't for Diversified increasing its price in period 2; Amalgamated wasn't higher-enough until it reached 1.06, relative to the 1.02.

Amalgamated raised its price once again in period 5 with its "Raise quality, raise price" non-strategy move. NSMs override strategies, and so Amalgamated went up even though it had already captured the high-price ground. This NSM simulates a more-than-enough price edge or another attempt to lead prices up.

Likewise, BigBiz cut its price in period 5 because it executed a "Raise quality, cut price" NSM. Perhaps BigBiz wanted to see if it could pick up a little more market share.

But BigBiz's action caused Consolidated and Diversified to change too. Consolidated was no longer sufficiently below its competitors to satisfy its desire to hold the lowest-price position, so it immediately cut its price to retaliate. Seeing Consolidated's swift reaction, BigBiz's managers might realize that further attempts to gain share might provoke a price war.

Diversified cut its price too, though its motives were a little more complex. Its chosen strategy tries to emulate the actions of its largest-share competitor. BigBiz had the biggest share in period 5; hence, when Diversified saw its exemplar cut price, it cut price too.

Why did BigBiz have the biggest share when Consolidated had lower prices? First, ValueWar measures market share by dollar sales, not unit sales, and a higher price per unit might produce a greater share even with lower unit sales.[1] More important, we'll soon see big disparities in quality. BigBiz's high quality more than offset Consolidated's low price.

---

[1] The tradeoff between unit sales and dollar sales depends on customers' sensitivity to price. In markets in which customers are very price sensitive, small differences in price can produce large differences in unit sales, and so low prices will tend to yield larger market shares. If customers aren't very price sensitive, then lower prices might not increase unit sales enough to compensate for the lower price per unit. Price sensitivity and quality sensitivity are controlled by scenario factors that you can alter with the ValueWar Calibrator software.

Note that BigBiz's managers may not know *why* two competitors decided to follow suit with their own price cuts. However, the instant counterstrike from Consolidated and Diversified would doubtless look like retaliation to BigBiz, which might consequently feel discouraged from further adventurism. Perhaps BigBiz should run another ValueWar simulation to see if they'd have been more profitable without their quickly neutralized experiment. You will see the results of running that test in Chapter 6.

After the brief flurry of adjustments in period 6, prices stay stable. Other combinations of strategies, of course, could lead to vastly different price patterns.

> **Note:** Relative prices tend to track absolute prices, but *a business's relative price can change even if the business takes no action*. For example, Amalgamated's relative price moved from 108 in period 5 to 109 in period 6 even though it held its absolute price at 1.08. Its relative price rose because two of its competitors' prices fell between periods 5 and 6. Thus, Amalgamated's products became less attractive, relative to its competitors', through no action of its own. Lesson: Watch your competitors!

Absolute quality and relative quality

	Absolute quality				Relative quality			
Per	A	B	C	D	A	B	C	D
0	70.0	70.0	70.0	70.0	100	100	100	100
1	72.0	72.0	68.0	70.0	102	102	96	99
2	74.0	74.0	66.0	72.0	103	103	92	101
3	76.0	76.0	66.0	74.0	104	104	90	101
4	78.0	78.0	66.0	76.0	105	105	89	102
5	80.0	80.0	66.0	78.0	105	105	87	103
6	82.0	82.0	68.0	80.0	105	105	87	103
7	84.0	84.0	70.0	82.0	105	105	88	103
8	86.0	86.0	72.0	84.0	105	105	88	102
9	88.0	88.0	74.0	86.0	105	105	88	102
10	90.0	90.0	76.0	88.0	105	105	88	102
11	92.0	92.0	78.0	90.0	105	105	89	102
12	94.0	94.0	80.0	92.0	104	104	89	102
13	95.0	95.0	82.0	94.0	104	104	90	103
14	95.0	95.0	84.0	95.0	103	103	91	103
15	95.0	95.0	85.0	95.0	103	103	92	103
16	95.0	95.0	85.0	95.0	103	103	92	103
17	95.0	95.0	85.0	95.0	103	103	92	103
18	95.0	95.0	85.0	95.0	103	103	92	103
19	95.0	95.0	85.0	95.0	103	103	92	103
20	95.0	95.0	85.0	95.0	103	103	92	103

ValueWar defines **absolute quality** as everything the customer cares about except for price. Thus, raising quality can mean improving basic performance, extending warranties, polishing the product's image, and so on. This notion of quality is a tremendously important and powerful competitive-strategy concept, but a full discussion of it is beyond the scope of this book.

Each business's **relative quality** is its absolute quality divided by the average of all the businesses' absolute qualities. If a business's relative quality measures over 100%, then its absolute quality is better than the average in the market.

ValueWar's simulations for absolute quality and relative quality work about the same way as the price simulations. Businesses directly influence their absolute quality, within limits set by scenario factors; their relative quality depends on their actions and on the actions of their competitors.

In the analysis we've developed so far, the pattern we see for quality differs considerably from the one we saw for price. Amalgamated and BigBiz declare war on each other immediately, as they've both chosen strategies that try to get the dominant level of quality in the market. They keep raising the ante on each other until they hit their limits on maximum-attainable quality in period 13.

Meanwhile, Diversified scores its own quality improvements because its strategy compels it to mimic its largest-share competitor, which turns out to be BigBiz. Since BigBiz raises its quality consistently, Diversified does so too.

Diversified always lags one period behind BigBiz. While BigBiz immediately jumped in and started to improve quality, Diversified's strategy made Diversified wait for one period to see what #1 would do. Though reactive strategies like Diversified's often produce good results, they rarely produce the best results.[1]

Consolidated takes the low road, cutting its quality from 70 to 68 to 66. It holds at 66 for a few periods because it's satisfied that it's lower than its competitors.

But in period 6 even Consolidated starts to improve its quality. It does so because it realizes (obeying a ValueWar factor; see the *Reference* section) that it would be suicide to persist at 66 while its competitors scored higher and higher. Consolidated stops improving in period 15 when its nearest competitor likewise stops improving.

Note that the changes in *absolute* quality far exceed the changes in *relative* quality, because (in this case) the competitors' strategies tend to make them move together. Despite all the skirmishes, no competitor emerges with a distinct quality advantage; only Consolidated ends up with a position clearly matching its original strategic intent.

Are the businesses in the Horse race better off with higher overall quality? The factors for this scenario make ValueWar raise costs when quality goes up, but demand accelerates when average quality rises, so they sell more and gain experience and scale economies. You could run simulations that keep quality steady so you could see whether greater demand and economies outweigh higher costs. And what if you could raise quality *without* raising costs...? ValueWar can simulate "quality is free" strategies via appropriate values for the cost of quality factors.

In the demo run, prices drop a bit even as quality rises, which would make market demand high. Other simulations could investigate whether one or more competitors would be well served by forgoing some growth for price increases to parallel the quality improvements.

---

[1] The follow-the-biggest strategy can lead to odd behavior. For example, say competitor A had the biggest share from period 1 through period 5, competitor B took the lead in period 6, and competitor C became #1 in period 14. If competitor D tried to emulate its biggest competitor, it would follow three different strategies over five years! Its performance might well suffer.

Market share and sales

	Market share				Sales			
Per	A	B	C	D	A	B	C	D
0	25.0	25.0	25.0	25.0	10000	10000	10000	10000
1	25.5	25.5	24.2	24.8	10388	10369	9827	10107
2	25.9	25.9	23.1	25.2	10786	10794	9615	10482
3	26.1	26.2	22.5	25.2	11084	11132	9571	10737
4	26.1	26.4	22.0	25.5	11349	11463	9570	11098
5	26.3	26.5	21.5	25.7	11680	11771	9552	11434
6	26.2	26.6	21.4	25.7	11835	12036	9679	11629
7	26.1	26.6	21.5	25.8	12060	12298	9960	11932
8	26.0	26.5	21.6	25.8	12338	12576	10247	12220
9	26.0	26.5	21.7	25.8	12621	12864	10538	12511
10	26.0	26.5	21.8	25.8	12910	13159	10835	12806
11	25.9	26.4	21.9	25.7	13203	13457	11135	13104
12	25.9	26.4	22.0	25.7	13507	13767	11445	13414
13	25.8	26.3	22.1	25.8	13718	13982	11786	13760
14	25.5	26.0	22.5	25.9	13835	14101	12190	14046
15	25.4	25.9	22.8	25.9	13982	14251	12530	14237
16	25.4	25.9	22.9	25.9	14168	14440	12749	14437
17	25.4	25.9	22.9	25.9	14372	14648	12946	14647
18	25.4	25.9	22.9	25.9	14581	14862	13138	14862
19	25.4	25.9	22.9	25.9	14793	15078	13329	15078
20	25.4	25.9	22.9	25.9	15010	15299	13525	15299

Each business's **market share** is its sales (in dollars, pounds, yen, etc.) divided by the market's total sales. **Sales** equal unit sales times absolute price.

Comparing sales and unit sales (on a subsequent page of the report) highlights the differences among the businesses' strategies. For example, Amalgamated's unit sales lag far behind its competitors', due to its premium price. Consolidated's sales suffer relative to unit sales because of its heavy discounting.

Businesses generally show increases in market share by selling more units than in a prior period. However, there are two ways in which a business can gain share while selling fewer units than it did before. One: The size of the market may have shrunk and the business's competitors' may have lost even more unit sales. Two: A price increase may raise sales even if unit sales decline.

Changes in market share depend on seven factors in ValueWar. All of these factors are controlled by scenario factors. Please refer to the *Reference* section of this book for more details.

- *Relative price.* All things being otherwise equal, customers usually prefer low prices to high. Hence, businesses with low relative prices will sell more units than those with high relative prices, all else being equal.

- *Relative quality*. All else equal, customers prefer high-quality products and services. Attaining a quality advantage — that is, high relative quality — will increase unit sales. Scenario factors control the extent to which customers respond to price and quality. Some markets are price sensitive; others care more about quality.

- *Perception time*. Customers might not immediately perceive competitors' changes in quality or price. In the Horse-race scenario they do, but other scenarios in the ValueWar demo simulate customers whose perceptions lag reality.

- *Customer loyalty*. ValueWar incorporates a factor to factor customer loyalty into market-share calculations. Specifically, a business will always retain a certain percentage of its customers from the previous period, even if its products become less attractive. (The percentage will be 0 in markets with no loyalty.) Incidentally, although the factor is called "loyalty," it also simulates switching costs.

- *Customer disloyalty*. The flip side of loyalty: a certain percentage of a business's customers might decide to try a competitor's product or service just for the sake of trying something new. These customers will switch even if the competitor's product or service is lower in quality than their current supplier's. The percentage of customers who exhibit this behavior is controlled by a scenario factor.

- *Eligibility*. ValueWar captures the effects of brand recognition, approved vendor lists, awareness, etc., in the eligibility factor. A business may have a fine product or service and it may have plenty of production capacity, but it may be limited in its sales because too few customers recognize its existence or consider it an acceptable vendor. (You'll find more detail in this chapter and in the *Reference* section.) In the Horse-race scenario, no competitor's sales are constrained by low eligibility.

- *Capacity*. A business cannot sell more than it can produce. Customers will switch to a competitor if their favorite supplier can't satisfy their demand. They'll then become loyal to their new supplier.

We see in the demo report that Consolidated's market share slid quickly from 25.0% to a low of 21.4% in period 6. This decline stems from two events: Consolidated's relative quality dropped faster than its relative price, causing customers to look elsewhere for better value, and its absolute price went down, causing sales to sag. After period 6, Consolidated's revived quality helped it rebuild some of the share it lost.

Amalgamated initially seems nearly unaffected by its escalating price. Immunized by its high quality, insulated by loyal customers, and assisted by defections from Consolidated, its share rose for about a year. But then it raised price further while BigBiz cut price in period 5, and Consolidated and Diversified made their own cuts in period 6, so Amalgamated lost some share in period 6. Then it's a slow slide as once-loyal but quality-insensitive customers trickle away. As we'll see, the changes in Amalgamated's unit share are more dramatic than in its market share.

BigBiz (and Diversified, one period later) set out to conquer the market. They gained share because their relative quality soared while relative prices dipped. Some of BigBiz's gains evaporated as Consolidated made up lost ground. Note that BigBiz gained more, then lost more, than Diversified, due to its more-aggressive actions. They end the simulation neck and neck.

Unit share and unit sales

	Unit share				Unit sales			
Per	A	B	C	D	A	B	C	D
0	25.0	25.0	25.0	25.0	10000	10000	10000	10000
1	25.0	25.5	24.6	24.8	10184	10369	10028	10107
2	25.0	26.0	24.2	24.8	10367	10794	10011	10277
3	24.6	26.3	23.8	25.3	10445	11132	10075	10737
4	24.7	26.5	23.2	25.6	10694	11463	10073	11098
5	24.4	27.1	22.7	25.8	10791	12011	10055	11434
6	24.0	27.0	22.9	26.1	10933	12282	10396	11867
7	24.0	26.9	23.0	26.1	11188	12549	10699	12175
8	24.0	26.9	23.0	26.1	11445	12833	11006	12470
9	23.9	26.8	23.1	26.1	11708	13127	11320	12766
10	23.9	26.8	23.2	26.1	11976	13427	11638	13067
11	23.9	26.8	23.3	26.1	12248	13732	11960	13372
12	23.8	26.7	23.4	26.0	12530	14048	12293	13687
13	23.7	26.6	23.6	26.2	12725	14267	12660	14041
14	23.5	26.3	24.0	26.2	12834	14389	13094	14332
15	23.4	26.2	24.3	26.2	12970	14542	13458	14527
16	23.3	26.2	24.3	26.2	13142	14735	13694	14731
17	23.3	26.2	24.3	26.2	13332	14947	13905	14946
18	23.3	26.2	24.3	26.2	13526	15165	14112	15165
19	23.3	26.2	24.3	26.2	13723	15385	14317	15385
20	23.3	26.2	24.3	26.2	13924	15611	14528	15611

Unit share is just like market share except that it's calculated on the basis of unit sales, not sales revenue. If all competitors in a market have the same prices, then unit share and market share will be equal.

In the report we've run, Amalgamated's unit share in period 20 is 23.3% and its market share is 25.4%. Its market share is higher than its unit share because it charges a premium price, meaning that it gets more sales per unit than its competitors get.

Unit sales refers to the number of units each business sold in each period. Unit sales times absolute price equals sales. Other relationships: unit sales divided by unit capacity equals capacity utilization; unit sales times variable costs per unit equals variable costs.

If a business has sufficient capacity, its unit sales will equal its unit demand. ValueWar will not allow a business to, in effect, exceed 100% capacity utilization: unit sales will equal unit demand or unit capacity, whichever is smaller. The businesses all have enough capacity to handle their unit demand with the strategies we've simulated in the *Tutorial*, so in this case unit sales always matches unit demand.

Unit sales will be less than unit demand if unit capacity is too small. But a business's unit sales can also exceed unit demand. This phenomenon will occur if one or more competitors hasn't enough capacity to fulfill its own demand, and if this business's capacity can pick up some of the slack. Unit sales from businesses' unmet demand will be parceled out to the competitors with sufficient capacity in proportion to the market shares they'd rate in a "mini market" in which the capacity-constrained businesses don't compete.[1] (In other words, customers buy from their "next-best" choice of supplier.) In the demo report, though, this situation never arises; unit capacity is always enough to meet demand, so unit sales always equals unit demand.

---

[1] ValueWar creates these mini markets, with fewer and fewer competitors, until all of the market's demand has been satisfied or no more capacity is available from any competitor.

Unit demand and eligibility

	Unit demand				Eligibility			
Per	A	B	C	D	A	B	C	D
0	10000	10000	10000	10000	100.0	100.0	100.0	100.0
1	10184	10369	10028	10107	100.0	100.0	100.0	100.0
2	10367	10794	10011	10277	100.0	100.0	100.0	100.0
3	10445	11132	10075	10737	100.0	100.0	100.0	100.0
4	10694	11463	10073	11098	100.0	100.0	100.0	100.0
5	10791	12011	10055	11434	100.0	100.0	100.0	100.0
6	10933	12282	10396	11867	100.0	100.0	100.0	100.0
7	11188	12549	10699	12175	100.0	100.0	100.0	100.0
8	11445	12833	11006	12470	100.0	100.0	100.0	100.0
9	11708	13127	11320	12766	100.0	100.0	100.0	100.0
10	11976	13427	11638	13067	100.0	100.0	100.0	100.0
11	12248	13732	11960	13372	100.0	100.0	100.0	100.0
12	12530	14048	12293	13687	100.0	100.0	100.0	100.0
13	12725	14267	12660	14041	100.0	100.0	100.0	100.0
14	12834	14389	13094	14332	100.0	100.0	100.0	100.0
15	12970	14542	13458	14527	100.0	100.0	100.0	100.0
16	13142	14735	13694	14731	100.0	100.0	100.0	100.0
17	13332	14947	13905	14946	100.0	100.0	100.0	100.0
18	13526	15165	14112	15165	100.0	100.0	100.0	100.0
19	13723	15385	14317	15385	100.0	100.0	100.0	100.0
20	13924	15611	14528	15611	100.0	100.0	100.0	100.0

Unit demand indicates the number of units that customers *want* to buy from each business. Unit sales will equal unit demand for each business that has enough production capacity to satisfy its demand.

If demand for a business's products or services exceeds its capacity (which doesn't happen in the demo report), then it will lose sales to its competitors. In other words, customers will switch to their second choice rather than wait for their favorite supplier to add capacity. They'll switch to their third or fourth choice if their second or third hasn't enough capacity either.

Adding the four competitors' unit demands (or capacities, on a subsequent page of the report) in any period yields the market's total demand (or supply). Market supply and demand appear on page 1 of the report.

Eligibility simulates brand recognition, awareness, approved vendor lists, limited access to distribution channels, and similar phenomena. ValueWar uses eligibility to show how customers in some markets are reluctant to buy from young, unstable, or "risky" businesses even if those businesses offer superior quality or aggressive prices. In effect, eligibility imposes a limit on market share.

In the Horse race, all the businesses are reputable and accepted, with 100% eligibility, so eligibility doesn't constrain any business's sales. (Specifically, the minimum-eligibility factor is set to 100% for all the businesses, so their eligibility never dips below 100%.)

Eligibility changes as a function of three factors. All of these factors are controlled by scenario factors. Please refer to the *Reference* section of this book for more details.

- *"Natural" growth over time*. By the very fact of surviving, businesses increase their eligibility. This factor captures increasing awareness or brand recognition due to repeated exposure, for example. It can also capture expanded access to distribution channels (the cost of which will normally be put into the various cost factors in the process of calibrating ValueWar for a business situation).

- *Increases in eligibility with increases in share of units sold.*[1] If unit market share rises, eligibility goes up. This relationship shows the "bandwagon" effect; in other words, it shows how acceptance by some customers makes a business more acceptable to other customers.

- *Decreases in eligibility with decreases in share of units sold.*[2] If unit share declines for a business, its eligibility may decline too. This effect simulates how competitors can fall out of favor. Losing a long-time customer, for example, might cause other customers to question the continued viability of the business.

You can see the values for these factors by summoning scenario information via the scenario-information section of the ValueWar help system (press (F1)). Like all other scenario factors, the three are calibrated to reflect a business's specific market conditions.

Each business's eligibility starts out at the level set by the initial-eligibility factor; changes in eligibility are bounded by the minimum-eligibility and maximum-eligibility factors. You can see these factors in the scenario-information help screens.

---

[1] ValueWar connects eligibility to unit sales, not to sales revenue, to prevent eligibility from being distorted by changes in prices.
[2] ValueWar uses separate increases-with-share and decreases-with-share factors because the two rates of change might be different in some markets.

Loyalty and unit capacity

	Loyalty				Unit capacity			
Per	A	B	C	D	A	B	C	D
0	25.0	25.0	25.0	25.0	12500	12500	12500	12500
1	25.0	25.0	25.0	25.0	12500	12500	12500	12500
2	25.0	25.0	25.0	25.0	12500	12500	12500	12500
3	25.0	25.0	25.0	25.0	12500	12500	12500	12500
4	25.0	25.0	25.0	25.0	12500	12737	12500	12500
5	25.0	25.0	25.0	25.0	12500	13346	12500	12704
6	25.0	25.0	25.0	25.0	12500	13647	12500	13185
7	25.0	25.0	25.0	25.0	12500	13943	12500	13528
8	25.0	25.0	25.0	25.0	12716	14259	12500	13855
9	25.0	25.0	25.0	25.0	13009	14585	12577	14185
10	25.0	25.0	25.0	25.0	13307	14919	12931	14519
11	25.0	25.0	25.0	25.0	13609	16250	13289	14858
12	25.0	25.0	25.0	25.0	13922	16250	13659	16250
13	25.0	25.0	25.0	25.0	14139	16250	14066	16250
14	25.0	25.0	25.0	25.0	14260	16250	14549	16250
15	25.0	25.0	25.0	25.0	14411	16250	14954	16250
16	25.0	25.0	25.0	25.0	14603	17500	16250	17500
17	25.0	25.0	25.0	25.0	14813	17500	16250	17500
18	25.0	25.0	25.0	25.0	16250	17500	16250	17500
19	25.0	25.0	25.0	25.0	16250	17500	16250	17500
20	25.0	25.0	25.0	25.0	16250	17500	16250	17500

Each business's **loyalty** reflects its percentage of loyal customers. These customers will stick with the business for the next period even if they "should" switch to one of its competitors. Thus, even if, say, BigBiz became horribly uncompetitive in period 4, it would retain 25% of its customers from period 4 to period 5. If it did nothing to remedy the situation in period 5, it would retain 25% of its remaining customers in period 6 (that is, just over 6% of its period-4 customer base).

It's rare for customers to totally abandon a business overnight, due to switching costs, the value of good relationships between salespeople and purchasers, and just plain inertia. ValueWar uses loyalty to capture these effects. The lower the loyalty, the more possible it is for customers to desert en masse; the higher the loyalty, the more they stick with a supplier through thick and thin (or through ignorance or iron-clad contracts or whatever).

Note that loyalty does *not* cover the time that it takes for customers to perceive changes in quality or price. ValueWar uses other factors that directly address those perception times.

Loyalty can change, depending on the factor that controls how changes in quality affect loyalty. When loyalty mainly reflects switching costs, changes in quality will have little if any effect on loyalty, so the loyalty-change-with-quality factor should be set to zero. However, when it is set to a non-zero value, then businesses that increase their absolute quality will find that their customers reward them with greater loyalty; likewise, businesses that drop their quality will find that their disappointed customers will be less loyal than in the past. Please refer to the *Reference* section of this book for more information.

Unit capacity indicates the number of units that each business can produce in one period. It changes over time depending on capacity additions, if any.

ValueWar implements two kinds of capacity additions: debottlenecking and "regular" capacity. The amount of each, and the points at which they can be added, are controlled by scenario factors.

Debottlenecking refers to adding capacity by improving the flow through the slowest parts of the production process. It can occur in any period; for example, BigBiz debottlenecks in period 4, thereby increasing its capacity from 12500 to 12737. However, opportunities to add capacity through debottlenecking are typically limited.

Regular capacity additions take place as often as needed (subject to limits controlled by scenario factors), but, since they usually take time, they cannot occur early in the simulation.

ValueWar makes a simplifying assumption about regular capacity additions, to wit, that businesses can forecast accurately when they'll need capacity and how long it'll take for them to add it. Thus, if it takes 8 periods (2 years) to build a plant, and if a business needs that plant in period 12, then ValueWar assumes that managers will decide in period 4 to build a plant and that the plant will be built by period 12.[1]

Debottlenecking and regular additions happen when capacity utilization (shown on the next page of the report) reaches a "trigger point." In the demo, all the businesses use 90% utilization as their trigger point, meaning that each will add enough capacity to keep its utilization at 90%. (You can see these numbers by requesting scenario information from the help system.) Trigger points below 100% indicate a reluctance to ever experience stockouts; points above 100% indicate a reluctance to add capacity that might go unused if sales turn down.

Capacity costs money; the amount depends on scenario factors. Businesses that add any kind of capacity will show corresponding increases in fixed costs.

Because ValueWar simulates just five years, it doesn't allow any business to scrap, sell, or transfer capacity it doesn't need any more.

---

[1] It is possible to approximate some effects of relaxing this assumption. If, for example, the capacity trigger point is set higher than normal, then ValueWar will delay capacity additions, an effect corresponding to adding capacity too late.

We will see in the demo report that BigBiz hits its target 90% utilization within 4 periods. Having done so, it debottlenecks, causing unit capacity to inch upward.

By period 8, three of the competitors have added capacity because they reached their 90% triggers. Consolidated, the laggard, hit 90% in period 9.

None of the businesses ran out of debottlenecking capacity before period 8; if any had, their utilization would have climbed over 90%. Regular capacity becomes available in period 9. No competitor hit capacity constraints in this simulation.

When a business exhausts its opportunities to debottleneck, ValueWar adds regular capacity in chunks that correspond to the business's minimum economic plant size. In this case, the chunk size is 10%, meaning that regular capacity additions boost capacity by 10% of each business's original 12,500-unit capacity. BigBiz adds its first chunk in period 11.[1]

---

[1] BigBiz did its last debottlenecking *and* completed its first new plant in period 11. Its unit demand in period 11 would have required utilizing over 90% of its period-10 capacity. But even with maximum debottlenecking — 20%, or going from 12,500 to 15,000 — utilization would still exceed its 90% trigger. So, BigBiz had to add 1,250 units of regular capacity for period 11.

Capacity utilization and cumulative units

	Capacity utilization				Cumulative units			
Per	A	B	C	D	A	B	C	D
0	80.0	80.0	80.0	80.0	250000	250000	250000	250000
1	81.5	83.0	80.2	80.9	260184	260369	260028	260107
2	82.9	86.3	80.1	82.2	270551	271163	270039	270384
3	83.6	89.1	80.6	85.9	280996	282295	280114	281121
4	85.6	90.0	80.6	88.8	291691	293758	290188	292220
5	86.3	90.0	80.4	90.0	302481	305770	300242	303654
6	87.5	90.0	83.2	90.0	313415	318052	310639	315520
7	89.5	90.0	85.6	90.0	324602	330601	321337	327696
8	90.0	90.0	88.0	90.0	336047	343434	332343	340165
9	90.0	90.0	90.0	90.0	347755	356561	343663	352931
10	90.0	90.0	90.0	90.0	359731	369988	355301	365998
11	90.0	84.5	90.0	90.0	371979	383720	367261	379370
12	90.0	86.4	90.0	84.2	384508	397768	379554	393058
13	90.0	87.8	90.0	86.4	397234	412035	392214	407099
14	90.0	88.5	90.0	88.2	410067	426424	405307	421431
15	90.0	89.5	90.0	89.4	423037	440965	418766	435958
16	90.0	84.2	84.3	84.2	436179	455700	432460	450690
17	90.0	85.4	85.6	85.4	449511	470647	446365	465636
18	83.2	86.7	86.8	86.7	463038	485812	460477	480801
19	84.4	87.9	88.1	87.9	476760	501198	474794	496186
20	85.7	89.2	89.4	89.2	490684	516809	489322	511797

Each business's **capacity utilization** is its unit sales divided by its unit capacity. Capacity utilization reflects not only sales performance for the four businesses but also the capacity decisions they make.

All the businesses managed to maintain close to 90% utilization because none lost market share precipitously, because they added capacity in relatively small chunks, and because the market grew at a healthy pace. Other markets can end up with widespread, horrendous overcapacity due to market-share crashes, enormous capacity additions, or recessions. Likewise, businesses in still other markets may find they can't satisfy demand in either the near term (because they can't debottleneck any more) or in the long term (because they can't add enough regular capacity).

See the discussion of unit capacity, from the previous page of the ValueWar report, for more comments that include capacity utilization.

Cumulative units indicates the number of units sold by each business up to and including each period. It includes units sold prior to the start of the simulation, as required by ValueWar's "experience-effect" calculations.

"Experience" grows with accumulated production volume. The extent of the experience effect on variable costs is one of ValueWar's scenario factors. It is 6% for the Horse-race scenario in the ValueWar demo, which means that variable costs decline 6% with each successive doubling of accumulated production.

ValueWar uses cumulative units to calculate the experience effect on variable costs. For example, Consolidated's cumulative units grew from 250,000 at the start of the simulation to 489,322 by period 20. Thus, with nearly one full doubling of cumulative units, Consolidated's variable costs in period 20 will be about 6% lower than they were in period 0 (exclusive of other effects on costs, such as productivity and changes in quality).

Cumulative sales and total costs

	Cumulative sales				Total costs			
Per	A	B	C	D	A	B	C	D
0	250000	250000	250000	250000	8000	8000	8000	8000
1	260388	260369	259827	260107	8116	8190	7941	8029
2	271173	271163	269442	270590	8232	8404	7866	8139
3	282258	282295	279013	281327	8308	8587	7878	8368
4	293607	293758	288583	292425	8455	8816	7865	8559
5	305287	305529	298135	303859	8541	9213	7846	8783
6	317122	317566	307814	315489	8647	9436	8021	9107
7	329182	329864	317774	327420	8801	9659	8184	9354
8	341519	342440	328021	339640	9003	9896	8350	9595
9	354141	355305	338560	352151	9225	10142	8536	9840
10	367051	368463	349395	364957	9453	10395	8783	10090
11	380254	381921	360530	378061	9686	11018	9034	10346
12	393761	395688	371974	391475	9929	11280	9295	10986
13	407479	409669	383760	405236	10080	11442	9580	11283
14	421313	423770	395951	419281	10137	11501	9912	11529
15	435295	438021	408480	433518	10212	11580	10165	11678
16	449462	452461	421229	447955	10311	12105	10668	12177
17	463834	467109	434175	462602	10422	12222	10783	12295
18	478415	481971	447313	477464	10949	12337	10890	12409
19	493208	497049	460643	492541	11018	12412	10958	12485
20	508218	512348	474168	507840	11089	12490	11028	12563

Cumulative sales indicates total sales up to and including each period. Cumulative sales equals cumulative units in period 0 because absolute prices start at 1.00 in the Horse-race scenario. As prices change, cumulative sales and cumulative units diverge.

Total costs include fixed costs plus variable costs in each period. Each competitor in the Horse-race demo starts off with 8000 in total costs in period 0.

Note that all four businesses' costs rise in almost every period (Consolidated's first five periods being the exception). These increases occur because all of them are engaging in activities that incur higher costs: growing unit sales, improving quality (which costs money under the operations strategies in this scenario), and/or expanding capacity. Operations strategies, expressed via various scenario factors, control the degree to which those activities increase costs.

Fixed costs and variable costs/unit

	Fixed costs				Variable costs/unit			
Per	A	B	C	D	A	B	C	D
0	4000	4000	4000	4000	0.40	0.40	0.40	0.40
1	4016	4016	3984	4000	0.40	0.40	0.39	0.40
2	4032	4032	3968	4016	0.41	0.41	0.39	0.40
3	4048	4048	3968	4032	0.41	0.41	0.39	0.40
4	4064	4113	3968	4048	0.41	0.41	0.39	0.41
5	4081	4253	3968	4106	0.41	0.41	0.39	0.41
6	4097	4332	3984	4220	0.42	0.42	0.39	0.41
7	4113	4410	4000	4308	0.42	0.42	0.39	0.41
8	4174	4493	4016	4392	0.42	0.42	0.39	0.42
9	4252	4579	4048	4478	0.42	0.42	0.40	0.42
10	4331	4666	4135	4565	0.43	0.43	0.40	0.42
11	4411	5120	4225	4654	0.43	0.43	0.40	0.43
12	4494	5206	4317	5120	0.43	0.43	0.40	0.43
13	4549	5262	4418	5223	0.43	0.43	0.41	0.43
14	4574	5287	4535	5333	0.43	0.43	0.41	0.43
15	4606	5319	4627	5416	0.43	0.43	0.41	0.43
16	4646	5779	5049	5846	0.43	0.43	0.41	0.43
17	4691	5823	5093	5890	0.43	0.43	0.41	0.43
18	5150	5862	5132	5929	0.43	0.43	0.41	0.43
19	5150	5862	5132	5929	0.43	0.43	0.41	0.43
20	5150	5862	5132	5929	0.43	0.42	0.41	0.42

Fixed costs include non-variable marketing costs, R&D expenses, maintenance and depreciation, and other expenses that don't depend on volume. Fixed costs plus total variable costs equals total costs.

Fixed costs can change as a function of three factors: productivity, changes in capacity, and changes in absolute quality. Scenario factors control how these factors affect fixed costs. Note that productivity and changes in absolute quality can cause fixed costs to rise or to fall, depending on how the factors are set ... i.e., depending on the environment you want to simulate with ValueWar.

Productivity programs can improve fixed costs over time. For example, efforts in TQM can substantially reduce overhead, thereby trimming fixed costs. Other factors, such as mandated investment in pollution-control equipment, can be simulated as "negative productivity" — that is, productivity that causes costs to rise, not fall — which is why ValueWar allows negative values for its productivity factors.

If a business adds capacity, its fixed costs rise. This relationship captures the operating and depreciation expenses associated with the new capacity. The point at which a business adds capacity depends on its capacity utilization, its capacity-utilization "trigger," and the time required to build capacity. In the Horse-race scenario, every business's operations strategy makes capacity decisions the same way: Add capacity when utilization reaches 90% and when no further debottlenecking is possible.[1] Because it takes these businesses 2 years to build a plant, no new capacity (other than debottlenecking) can come on-stream until period 9 or later.

Changes in quality can, depending on the scenario, affect fixed costs as well as variable costs. This relationship simulates the cost of improving quality by, for example, replacing old machines with new, higher-precision equipment. It also simulates other fixed-cost means of improving quality, such as increasing advertising budgets.[2]

Over the first few periods we see that Amalgamated and BigBiz exhibit rising fixed costs, Diversified follows BigBiz with a one-period time delay, and Consolidated drives its costs down. This pattern mirrors each business's changes in absolute quality.

BigBiz diverges a bit from Amalgamated in period 4, its fixed costs going to 4113 while Amalgamated's rise only to 4064. The difference comes from BigBiz's slight increase in capacity (from debottlenecking) in period 4. The differences grow in subsequent periods as BigBiz adds still more capacity.

BigBiz and Diversified have major increases in fixed costs during year 3, and Consolidated a little later, because they expanded their capacity. After period 8 even Amalgamated adds some capacity, thereby adding some costs.

Variable costs/unit are per-unit production and distribution costs. Variable costs/unit change as a function of "experience," productivity, and changes in absolute quality. Scenario factors — that is, operations strategies — control how much variable costs depend on these factors. Note that productivity and changes in absolute quality can cause variable costs/unit to rise or to fall, depending on the values to which those factors are set ... that is, depending on the environment you're simulating with ValueWar.

Experience refers to a business's ability to make units cheaper as its cumulative production grows. Thus, businesses that increase their unit sales (by being in growth markets, by gaining market share, or both) tend to reduce their variable costs per unit.

Productivity programs can improve variable costs over time. For example, efforts in TQM can substantially reduce wastage of materials. Other factors, such as mandatory inspections or

---

[1] You can see these numbers by requesting "scenario information" from the help system.
[2] Scenario factors can control tradeoffs between improving quality via variable costs and fixed costs. You could explore the relative merits of each side of the tradeoff by customizing several scenarios, one in which quality changes affect only variable costs, one in which quality changes affect only fixed costs, and one in which quality changes affect both. The demonstration version of ValueWar has quality affect both variable and fixed costs, as you can see by calling up the scenario-information screens from the help menu.

pollution-control equipment, can be simulated as "negative productivity" — that is, productivity that causes costs to rise, not fall — which is why ValueWar allows negative values for its productivity factors.

Changes in absolute quality cause corresponding changes in variable costs/unit. For example, the Horse-race scenario is calibrated to make costs rise when quality rises, on the assumption that improving quality requires some expenditure — e.g., on finer raw materials — and that cutting quality generally allows shaving costs.[1] Quality changes have a more or less parallel effect on fixed costs, as discussed earlier.

We see that Amalgamated's variable costs/unit rise slowly but steadily through the first three years of the simulation, a result of its quality-improvement program. With comparable changes in quality, BigBiz's variable costs rise too. BigBiz's variable costs decline as of period 20, which reflects the fact that BigBiz sells more units (and thus accumulates more experience) than does Amalgamated. Diversified follows BigBiz fairly closely.

Consolidated's variable costs head down immediately, a consequence of modest growth in unit sales and of substantial cuts in quality. Its costs rise again starting in period 9 because, as discussed above, it has to play catch-up in quality.

So, by the time five simulated years have elapsed, we see that the market's cost structure has evolved considerably:

- Amalgamated has kept its fixed costs relatively low by pursuing the high-quality, high-price niche in the market, which in turn kept its capacity needs nominal. Its variable costs/unit, on the other hand, rose nearly 10% because of the costs it incurred to maintain high quality.

- BigBiz and Diversified have gone for volume, raising quality without raising prices. As a result, they needed to add large chunks of capacity. Their fixed and variable costs went up because of their enhanced quality, but the extra experience they acquired through their sales volume kept their variable costs/unit from getting out of hand.

- Consolidated set its sights on the low-quality, low-price end of the market. Its diminished quality helped it cut both variable and fixed costs, at least until it had to

---

[1] Some people believe that quality is profitable. They concentrate on TQM (total quality management), improvements in production and management processes, and requiring defect-free components from suppliers. Higher quality can also yield repeat purchases, which are more profitable than initial or trial purchases.

ValueWar accommodates the quality-is-profitable perspective, the quality-costs-money perspective, and anything in between. It can do so by applying appropriate values for scenario factors. For example, factors control the degree to which variable and fixed costs change with changes in quality. These factors can be set to 0, which tells ValueWar that improving quality doesn't cost anything. They can be set to negative numbers, which means that improving quality *saves* money. Another factor controls customer preferences for quality and price. If customers care more about quality than price, then strategies that improve quality and raise price will indeed produce higher profits than those that keep quality down.

build its quality back up to keep from falling too far behind its competitors. Even after rejuvenating its quality, Consolidated led the market in variable costs/unit in every period. And, as we will soon see, its overall unit costs were the lowest in the market.

The businesses' different cost structures gives them different incentives. With high variable costs/unit and low fixed costs, Amalgamated should care a bit more about price than about volume. Conversely, BigBiz and Diversified have substantially higher fixed costs than the others, so they care more about volume than price.

At the start of the simulation, all four competitors saw the world in the same way. But their different strategies, and their consequential differences in performance, give them new — and different — perspectives. These new perspectives would change their basic motives and objectives. Assuming that they care about the same things in year 4 as they did in year 1 would be a serious strategic blunder.

Understanding each others' motives would help them assess each others' strengths and weaknesses and even predict how each other might behave in the future. For example, Consolidated might figure that Amalgamated would consider itself sorely provoked by price cuts, even though price cuts would seem entirely rational to Consolidated. Likewise, BigBiz could infer that Amalgamated would happily follow price increases, whereas Consolidated would likely hold its prices, seeing a price advantage as an opportunity to expand its sales volume.

Total variable costs and relative costs/unit

	Total variable costs				Relative costs/unit			
Per	A	B	C	D	A	B	C	D
0	4000	4000	4000	4000	100.0	100.0	100.0	100.0
1	4100	4174	3957	4029	100.5	99.6	99.8	100.1
2	4200	4372	3898	4123	100.8	98.9	99.8	100.6
3	4260	4538	3910	4336	101.7	98.6	100.0	99.7
4	4391	4703	3897	4511	101.6	98.9	100.4	99.1
5	4460	4960	3878	4677	101.9	98.7	100.5	98.9
6	4550	5104	4038	4886	102.1	99.2	99.6	99.1
7	4687	5249	4184	5046	101.8	99.7	99.0	99.5
8	4828	5403	4334	5203	102.0	100.0	98.3	99.7
9	4973	5564	4489	5362	102.1	100.2	97.8	99.9
10	5122	5729	4647	5525	102.2	100.2	97.7	99.9
11	5275	5898	4809	5692	101.3	102.8	96.8	99.1
12	5435	6075	4978	5866	100.5	101.8	95.9	101.8
13	5531	6181	5162	6059	100.4	101.7	96.0	101.9
14	5562	6214	5377	6197	100.3	101.5	96.1	102.1
15	5606	6262	5538	6262	100.2	101.4	96.1	102.3
16	5665	6326	5619	6331	97.7	102.3	97.0	102.9
17	5731	6399	5690	6405	97.8	102.3	97.0	102.9
18	5799	6474	5758	6480	100.8	101.3	96.1	101.9
19	5868	6550	5826	6556	100.8	101.3	96.1	101.9
20	5939	6628	5896	6633	100.8	101.3	96.1	101.9

Variable costs/unit times unit sales equals **total variable costs**.

We saw above that variable costs/unit rose in some periods for some competitors and fell in other periods. *Total* variable costs rise in every period for every competitor, however, except for Consolidated's first 5 periods. This pattern indicates the rises in unit sales and absolute quality more than offset any per-unit declines in variable costs. If we looked only at total variable costs, though, we wouldn't know that some competitors are scoring per-unit cost reductions that may strengthen their competitive positions and financial performance.

Relative costs/unit shows each business's total costs per unit sold, relative to the average of all the businesses' total costs per unit. Thus, relative costs furnish a measure of competitive advantage and disadvantage similar to relative price and relative quality.

As we saw earlier, each competitor in the demo starts off with 8000 in total costs. Since each has the same total costs and the same unit sales in period 0, each has relative costs per unit of 100%.

We see some interesting trends in relative costs. Notice, for example, that BigBiz shows declining relative costs for most of the first year. By looking at other pages in the report we could trace that drop to spreading fixed costs over greater unit sales. Consolidated also shows lower relative costs, though partly for a different reason: lower variable costs per unit due to lower product quality.

Amalgamated's relative costs rise on and off until period 10 because it improves quality (which adds to costs in the Horse-race scenario) while raising prices (which depresses unit sales). Its low unit sales help keep costs *down* after period 10, however, because it doesn't need to add much capacity, unlike its competitors. Its costs are nearly the lowest until it adds capacity in year 5.

Amalgamated's experience reinforces an important point about relative unit costs. As with the other relative measures, a business's relative costs depend on its competitors' actions as much as on its own. Amalgamated's relative costs declined because its competitors' costs increased faster than did its own costs.

Amalgamated's experience illustrates another important principle as well. Though Amalgamated has the lowest unit sales and the least production capacity, it achieved very competitive unit costs.

Profit and return on sales (ROS)

	Profit				Return on sales			
Per	A	B	C	D	A	B	C	D
0	2000	2000	2000	2000	20.0	20.0	20.0	20.0
1	2272	2179	1886	2079	21.9	21.0	19.2	20.6
2	2553	2389	1749	2343	23.7	22.1	18.2	22.4
3	2776	2546	1693	2370	25.0	22.9	17.7	22.1
4	2894	2648	1705	2540	25.5	23.1	17.8	22.9
5	3140	2558	1706	2651	26.9	21.7	17.9	23.2
6	3188	2600	1658	2523	26.9	21.6	17.1	21.7
7	3260	2639	1777	2578	27.0	21.5	17.8	21.6
8	3335	2680	1897	2626	27.0	21.3	18.5	21.5
9	3396	2722	2002	2671	26.9	21.2	19.0	21.4
10	3457	2764	2053	2716	26.8	21.0	18.9	21.2
11	3517	2440	2101	2758	26.6	18.1	18.9	21.1
12	3578	2487	2150	2428	26.5	18.1	18.8	18.1
13	3638	2539	2206	2478	26.5	18.2	18.7	18.0
14	3698	2599	2279	2516	26.7	18.4	18.7	17.9
15	3770	2670	2364	2559	27.0	18.7	18.9	18.0
16	3856	2335	2081	2260	27.2	16.2	16.3	15.7
17	3950	2426	2163	2353	27.5	16.6	16.7	16.1
18	3632	2525	2248	2453	24.9	17.0	17.1	16.5
19	3775	2665	2371	2593	25.5	17.7	17.8	17.2
20	3921	2809	2497	2736	26.1	18.4	18.5	17.9

Now we get to the financial bottom line. In accordance with generally accepted accounting principles, **profit** equals dollar sales minus total costs.

Return on sales (ROS) is profit divided by sales. It helps you distinguish between rising profits and rising profitability. For example, the strategies we've simulated have caused profits to rise for all four competitors, but only one of them, Amalgamated, has raised its *rate* of profit generation.

Amalgamated's strategy is clearly successful. Its profits go up immediately and consistently; after 5 years, it earns close to double its initial profit per period: 3,921 versus 2,000. Some of that improvement doubtless comes from its growing sales (which came solely from market growth, since we saw that Amalgamated lost unit share). However, it also boosted its ROS (return on sales) from 20.0% to 26.1%. So, even after taking market growth into account, we can con-clude that Amalgamated's strategy, *when played against the strategies we selected for its competitors*, produced a steady stream of profits and profit growth.

For the first two years it looked as though BigBiz's and Diversified's profits would always grow steadily, with Diversified running close behind. But in period 11 BigBiz had to add a chunk of capacity, which interrupted its string of profits. Diversified's triumph over BigBiz was short-lived because it hit the same hiccup in period 12. BigBiz and Diversified continue to hit speed bumps as they ratchet up their capacity.

After 20 periods, BigBiz and Diversified both earn about 40% more than they did in period 0. However, their *rates* of profitability declined somewhat, to 18.4% and 17.9%, respectively.

Consolidated scored the smallest profit improvement. It took a risky approach, essentially trying to bribe customers into buying an inferior product. In fact, if it hadn't changed course to prevent its product from getting intolerably shoddy, its performance might never have shown any improvement. Consolidated's bottom line: profits rose about 20%, and profitability lower than the start (18.5% ROS).

BigBiz, Consolidated, and Diversified added capacity relatively early in accordance with their 90% trigger points, which caused their profits to fall. Obviously, their performance would have been considerably better had their trigger points been higher. A higher trigger point would be appropriate only if they could really operate at or near 100% utilization over the long term.

Amalgamated's profits rose while adding debottlenecking capacity; they dipped but recovered quickly even after expanding regular capacity in period 18. The simple reason: Amalgamated was profitable enough to make money even after absorbing the cost of its debottlenecking capacity.

One drag on profits was gone once the businesses called an end to their quality war in year 4. Their quality improvements had stimulated customer demand, but they had also kindled cost increases. Note that we'd have seen very different results if we'd simulated quality increases that *reduce* costs, especially if just one or two competitors would get that benefit.

It is very important to remember that results for all the competitors depend on the interaction among their strategies. Changing one business's strategy can change everyone's performance. We'll explore some such contingencies in Chapter 6.

And different strategies leave the businesses vulnerable to different events. For example, if a business had managed to swipe some share from Amalgamated after period 9, Amalgamated's performance might not suffer much because its fixed costs were low. Stealing share from high-cost BigBiz around period 11, on the other hand, could turn its rather successful expansion into an expensive boondoggle.

Note that the virtues of Amalgamated's strategy didn't become apparent for some time. It ran roughly even with BigBiz and Diversified for about a year … and then left them in the dust. And its success wasn't the result of a last-minute strategic flip; it came instead from steady pursuit of a clear strategic objective. Amalgamated's success illustrates the overwhelming importance of looking more than a year or two into the future when you plot your business's strategy!

It can be quite valuable to examine each business's trend in profit or cumulative profits. For example, does a competitor have to defer profits for a long time? If so, and if that competitor turns out to be impatient, you can expect a change in strategy. You can be even more sure that a change will come if that competitor observes other businesses earning respectable profits while it languishes in the doldrums.

Cumulative profits

```
     Cumulative profits
Per     A        B        C        D
---  --------  --------  --------  --------
 0     2000     2000     2000     2000

 1     4272     4179     3886     4079
 2     6825     6568     5635     6422
 3     9602     9114     7328     8792
 4    12496    11761     9033    11331

 5    15635    14320    10739    13982
 6    18823    16920    12397    16505
 7    22083    19559    14173    19082
 8    25418    22239    16070    21708

 9    28814    24961    18072    24379
10    32271    27725    20125    27095
11    35788    30165    22226    29853
12    39366    32651    24376    32281

13    43003    35190    26582    34759
14    46701    37790    28860    37275
15    50471    40460    31225    39834
16    54328    42795    33306    42094

17    58278    45221    35469    44446
18    61910    47746    37717    46899
19    65685    50412    40088    49492
20    69606    53220    42586    52228
```

Cumulative profits shows a running total of profits. Diversified earned 2,000 and 2,079 in periods 0 and 1, so its cumulative profit in period 1 was 4,079.

Cumulative profits measures the amount of money that each business earned over the course of the ValueWar simulation. By this metric, Amalgamated gets the gold. Its 69,606 total is a good 30% above BigBiz, the next-best performer.

Most managers intellectually prefer profit-oriented measures, such as cumulative profits, and would say that Amalgamated "won" this simulation. (The idea that "winning" means "beating the competition" is an assumption implicit in many strategies, and one that has tremendous long-term consequences. Discussing those consequences is beyond the scope of this book.)

But many managers use measures of success that focus on market share or unit share when they assess their performance. By that metric, Amalgamated "lost." Do you think they did? Would your colleagues agree?

Analyzing ValueWar

This chapter takes up where Chapter 5 left off. It explores the strategy implications of what we've seen so far, and it shows findings from additional ValueWar simulations.

Although the extra simulations are not shown in the *Tutorial*, they were run with the same competitors in the same market under the same constraints and factors as the simulation detailed above. You can replicate the simulations — and you can embellish them further with simulations of your own — with your demonstration copy of ValueWar.

The first half of this chapter discusses some principles of business strategy in context of the specific scenario we've simulated. The issues presented here certainly apply to other markets … in which they may have very different solutions!

The second half of this chapter introduces several kinds of advanced analysis you can perform with ValueWar, including some you can run with the demonstration version of the software. In particular, it discusses how you can use scenarios to address questions of operations strategies; that is, strategy questions concerning costs, uncertainties about the market, and so on.

Summary of the *Tutorial* analysis

Amalgamated won the most-profitable title. It raked in the most money by all three measures of profit (profit, return on sales, and cumulative profits). Moreover, Amalgamated played well in every period. Its consistent record both makes its market strategy desirable and encourages its managers to stick with it.

By the end of the five-year simulation, Amalgamated's three adversaries are operating under thinner margins than before, and an analysis of their cost structures (or more runs with Value-War) would show that they are more vulnerable than Amalgamated to bad news. Two have fixed costs nearly 20% higher than Amalgamated's, none has a quality edge over Amalgamated, and none is in a strong position to win a price war.

Of course, we might challenge Amalgamated's apparent victory on other grounds. We might prefer a measure of success other than ROS; or, we might, on further analysis, find that Amalgamated's strategy is the most risky in the sense that it could be sensitive to changes to the environment (e.g., increases in customers' sensitivity to price) or changes in competitors' strategies.

> Note that the virtues of Amalgamated's strategy didn't become apparent for some time. It ran roughly even with BigBiz and Diversified for a year ... and then left them in the financial dust. The high probability of encountering outcomes of this kind makes it even more important to simulate several years into the future.

Of course, Amalgamated can't do well by itself; its competitors have to "cooperate" by, for example, not embroiling the whole market in a price war. *Would* its competitors cooperate?

We assume that a "rational" competitor seeks benefits for itself and that it wouldn't take an action that would hurt Amalgamated at its own expense. Similarly, if a "rational" competitor finds itself in trouble, we assume it will act even if its action harms Amalgamated. So, we must investigate how well Amalgamated's competitors fare to see whether they have an incentive to cooperate.

Alternatively, we could see whether Amalgamated is in a position to reap its rewards even if its competitors *don't* cooperate. In other words, we could determine whether Amalgamated has become sufficiently powerful to ignore its competitors' actions, or whether it can compel its competitors to act in ways beneficial to its own performance. But we'll explore cooperation first.

All the competitors prosper for the first year or so. Only Consolidated's road holds any rocks, and they'd be more aptly described as pebbles. Managers in each business would have good reason to believe that they're doing well.

Year two brings a moment (a year?) of truth because that's when capacity starts to come on stream, causing profits to stagnate and ROS to decay. Debottlenecking comes first, followed by regular capacity. Remember that the *decisions* to add regular capacity came much earlier; it just took 8 periods to build the capacity.

Managers have three basic options when they run out of capacity:

- Add capacity (bring supply up to demand). Absorb the higher costs with increased sales. Generate higher profits, though not necessarily higher ROS. Acknowledge the possibility that a decline in demand can leave capacity underutilized. Accumulate production experience; the improved productivity translates into greater cost competitiveness.

- Raise prices and/or cut quality (bring demand down to supply). Skim the customers who are most profitable to the business. Keep rates of return high, but put an implicit cap — perhaps not immediately — on levels of profit. Run the risk that competitors will drive costs down at a faster rate and that they'll be better able to survive a price war.

- Turn away customers; don't change capacity, quality, or price (let supply and demand differ). There's not much point to this option, so ValueWar doesn't simulate it. However, ValueWar does provide a strategy — P(rice) by supply/demand — that simulates raising prices when demand is high and cutting prices when demand is low.

The market and operations strategies pursued by BigBiz, Consolidated, and Diversified call for increasing capacity. Do any of them have an incentive to switch market strategy ... that is, to subdue demand instead of expanding supply?

In a real-life analysis, managers would probably know quite a bit about their competitors' predilections and biases. They could contemplate whether the apparent risks and rewards shown by the simulation would suffice to make their competitors react. For now, all we have are the numbers.

The numbers indicate that none of the businesses has to make significant sacrifices and that all of them can continue to report growth and profits. Amalgamated might infer, therefore, that BigBiz, Consolidated, and Diversified would not feel a strong need to change gears. They'd likely feel satisfied that their strategies were performing as they had intended.

Thus, Amalgamated could conclude that its strategy, given its assumptions about what its competitors would do, would work quite well. Its analysis isn't complete yet, however, despite coming to this important conclusion. For example, Amalgamated should consider the possibility of "cheating." And, as noted above, we still have to contemplate the chances that Amalgamated may grow powerful enough to shape its competitors' actions so as to guarantee its own good results.

"Cheating"

The market evolution we've simulated with ValueWar included non-strategy moves (NSMs) in period 5. These actions effectively examined the consequences of Amalgamated and BigBiz trying to "cheat" a little: Amalgamated inched its price up a bit, and BigBiz cut its price a bit, even though they had both reached price points that satisfied their market-strategy objectives.

Did their cheating work? Well, we saw that Consolidated and Diversified reacted immediately, cutting their prices in period 6. BigBiz would see that its price cut had been neutralized, and it might conclude that further cuts would meet with similarly swift retribution.

Amalgamated wouldn't know *why* Consolidated and Diversified cut their prices; it wouldn't know whether they had responded to its price hike or to BigBiz's cut. It would certainly notice, however, that Consolidated and Diversified (as well as BigBiz) had cut their prices, and that those actions had cost it some of its market share.

6/ Analyzing ValueWar

We can run another ValueWar simulation to test the hypothesis that Amalgamated and BigBiz — and perhaps even Consolidated and Diversified — would be better off by not cheating. To do so, we just re-run their strategies without the period-5 NSMs.[1]

The result: three of the four businesses perform significantly better without the cheating. The fourth, Amalgamated, has a slight degradation in its financial performance, mitigated by a stronger market share.

Here we contrast cheating and no-cheating in period 20:

	Cumulative profits		Return on sales	
	Cheat	Don't cheat	Cheat	Don't cheat
Amalgamated	69,606	68,304	26.1%	26.1%
BigBiz	53,220	56,957	18.4	20.1
Consolidated	42,586	45,408	18.5	20.2
Diversified	52,228	55,647	17.9	19.3

Here's what caused the differences in performance:

- Amalgamated didn't end up at such a price disadvantage, so it didn't lose as much share. However, its slightly lower price per unit meant slightly lower profits. The bottom line: exemplary total profits and the best ROS, but trading some ROS for market share.

- BigBiz, Consolidated, and Diversified had a mirror image of Amalgamated's experience. Resisting the urge to cheat and retaliate left them with higher prices and higher relative prices, costing them a little market share but rewarding them with substantially better financial performance.

It appears that the no-cheating simulation generally provides better results and a more-stable environment than does the cheating simulation. You might want to try further tests, such as these:

- What would happen if Amalgamated or BigBiz cheats alone?

- What would happen if BigBiz "atones" and restores its price after Consolidated and Diversified strike back?

- What would happen if Amalgamated sees its competitors cutting prices, panics, and cuts its own price?

- What would happen if Consolidated misreads Diversified's intentions, concludes that Diversified is attacking it in the low-price segment, and executes a pre-emptive price cut?

---

[1] The results aren't shown here, but you can run them with your copy of the ValueWar demo.

Doing well versus doing better

We've seen that all the businesses can do well with the strategies we've simulated. A very different question: could they do *better* with different market or operations strategies?

But what is "better"? One set of strategies is clearly better than another if every business makes more money under the first set than under the second. But what if three of the businesses improve and one gets worse, even if only a little? What if one of the businesses performs much better while the other three show only minuscule improvements? What if a new set of strategies merely diminishes the likelihood of one competitor cheating, thereby improving the likelihood that another business will do well?

There is no "right" answer to these questions. Nonetheless, ValueWar provides us with the competitive data we need to understand who might gain (and by how much) and who might lose (and by how much). Thus informed, we can better predict how competitors will behave under various circumstances.

As a base-line case, we ran a ValueWar simulation for the Horse-race scenario with all four businesses following a "Don't change Q or P" market strategy. This analysis depicts what would happen if none of the businesses does anything, which amounts to a don't-rock-the-boat mentality.

	Cumulative profits		Return on sales	
	Strategy	Base-line	Strategy	Base-line
Amalgamated	69,606	62,475	26.1%	28.9%
BigBiz	53,220	62,475	18.4	28.9
Consolidated	42,586	62,475	18.5	28.9
Diversified	52,228	62,475	17.9	28.9

("Strategy" refers to the strategy combination developed during the Tutorial.
"Base-line" refers to the no-changes simulation.)

The four businesses show identical results under the base-line simulation because they start from identical positions and pursue identical market strategies. And the don't-change strategies perform identically well! Or maybe we should say that the original strategies led to poorer profits.

Why did the base-line set perform so well? One reason: no quality war broke out, so the competitors didn't have to increase costs. Of course, lower overall quality means lower overall demand; the base-line set yielded market-wide demand of 53,529 units in period 20, versus 59,674 in the original set. But the restrained demand has a silver lining in that it takes less capacity to satisfy, which improves profitability.

Note that at least one other set of market strategies can produce the same results. In the base-line set each business ignores its competitors; if each business followed the "tit for best tat" strategy, each would wait for another to flinch first. But in other ways these two strategy sets are critically different. You might enjoy experimenting with occasional "cheating" (NSMs) under the no-change set and under the don't-flinch-first set.

If you have the ValueWar Calibrator you might enjoy experimenting with the results of these market strategies when they're coupled with different operations strategies. What effect would cheating have if the cheater had a significantly better cost structure than its competitors? Such a competitor could afford the risk more than could the competitors with cost disadvantages.

Opportunism

Other than slicing 10% off one measure of Amalgamated's performance, the base-line, no-changes strategy set clearly looks better than the strategy set we simulated through the *Tutorial*. But what if one business decides to risk its competitors' wrath and make a brazen move? And what if its competitors decide they have to respond in kind, thus escalating the battle?

The answer depends entirely on the direction that the daring business takes.

If the opportunistic one moves quality and price up, for example, it could usher in the golden age of horse races, especially if other businesses follow it up. Customers in this market would will-ingly pay higher prices for better products, and the higher prices handily offset the costs of improving quality. It's possible for financial performance to almost double that of the base-line.

If, however, the opportunistic one spooks its competitors into following quality and price down-ward, then the market falls into a tailspin. Yes, lower price stimulates demand, but lower quality dampens demand. The net effect of this strategic mud wrestling: lower prices for everyone, no competitive advantages, and profits less than half of what they'd have been if everyone had left well enough alone.

The table below simulates the results of every competitor holding still, moving quality and price up, or pushing quality and price down.

	Cumulative profits		
	Don't change Q or P	Highest Q and P	Lowest Q and P
Amalgamated	62,475	114,595	24,558
BigBiz	62,475	114,595	24,558
Consolidated	62,475	114,595	24,558
Diversified	62,475	114,595	24,558

Implications for each competitor: follow the market up, and don't court disaster.

Have it your way

We mentioned above that Amalgamated should consider whether it can arrange its environment — that is, its position relative to its competitors — so that it can shape events to work toward Amalgamated's benefit.

This question is difficult but important. It is clear in real life that some competitors have more clout than others, and it is clear that the actions of a dominant competitor can compel others to make moves they might not otherwise make. A major new product, for example, or a major price change from the number-one player in a market practically forces the others to respond in some way.

You can analyze Amalgamated's (or any other competitor's) competitive advantage, in part with ValueWar, and in part outside it.

Some scenarios can reflect greater or lesser clout among competitors. High levels of customer loyalty, for example, tend to make competitors more independent of the others' actions. Greater flexibility in capacity indicates a competitor might have leverage over the others, since it can benefit more than the others from actions that increase demand and total profits at the expense of per-unit profits. Wider latitude in price or quality can have a similar effect: the competitor who can price the lowest can "win," in a sense, a price war.

These factors (loyalty, capacity, and so on) are part of ValueWar's scenarios. Make multiple scenarios with different values for those factors; analyze the effects of strategies across scenarios (use the scenario sensitivity test) to test the competitive-clout issue.

You can also analyze competitive advantage by the probabilities you assign to competitors adopting certain strategies. You might discover that a certain combination of strategies works well for one competitor and poorly for others, for example; if you think the lucky competitor is powerful in its market, then you might weigh those outcomes highly, whereas if you think the lucky competitor is not so influential, then you might give the outcomes corresponding low probabilities of ever coming to pass.

The idea of competitive clout is both important and complex. Experiment with ValueWar simulations — and with your interpretations of those simulations — and you may get results that are provocative at the very least!

Strategy and uncertainty

Uncomfortable and undesirable it may be, but uncertainty about the future is undeniable and unavoidable.

The classic example: market growth. Every manager wants to know how fast his or her business's market will grow over in the future because that growth will influence decisions ranging from capacity additions to advertising budgets.

Unfortunately, managers often use dangerous techniques for dealing with uncertain growth. For example, planning for best-case growth is clearly risky. Making massive investment only to see the market evaporate is a well-traveled road to ruin.

Planning for worst-case growth seems like a prudent alternative; it avoids risk by avoiding lavish spending and has an air of responsibility and prudence. But worst-case strategies run risks of their own: they are usually suboptimal for outcomes other than the worst case, and they may even be fatally suboptimal if the timidity they produce lets bolder competitors run away with the market. In other words, fiduciary conservatism may lead to a competitive rout.

ValueWar does not predict market growth. However, it can help you determine whether uncertainty about market growth matters for your strategy decisions. Should you select one strategy if you assume fast growth and a different strategy if you assume slow growth? How much potential upside might you have to sacrifice to prevent a catastrophe?

There's a set of scenarios on your ValueWar demonstration disk that lets you experiment with this dilemma. You can duplicate the analyses shown here, and run some of your own, by starting ValueWar with the command VW GROWTH. This command uses a set of scenarios designed to illustrate the growth-uncertainty problem.

There are three scenarios in this run:

- Horse race, which is identical to the Horse race scenario we've used throughout the *Tutorial*.

- Horse race (lo grow), which is just like Horse race but with a 1.0% annual growth rate instead of the 6.0% in Horse race.

- Horse race (hi grow), which is also just like Horse race, but with a 10% growth rate.

We'll focus first on the Horse race scenario we've used so far, and we'll focus on Amalgamated. Remember that you can use the ValueWar help system to look at the differences in the scenarios: press (F1) to enter the help system, then select scenario information. The only differences in these three scenarios is in the market factors screen that shows growth rates. (Press (→) to get to that screen, then (PGUP) or (PGDN) to move among the scenarios.)

If you want to run these analyses yourself, select these strategies:

- Amalgamated... Raise Q and P.
- BigBiz............... Highest Q, steady P.
- Consolidated .... Steady Q, lowest P
- Diversified .... Lowest Q and P.

If you look at cumulative profits in period 20 (we will assume that cumulative profits is our key measure of success), you will find these results: Amalgamated, 72,223; BigBiz, 56,679; Consolidated, 18,521; and Diversified, 17,745. We will assume no changes in strategy for the purposes of this discussion.

Now run a scenario test (press (F5)) and look at cumulative profits in period 20. Here's what you'll see:

	Cumulative profits			
	Amalgamated	BigBiz	Consolidated	Diversified
Horse race (lo grow)	56,202	48,545	15,499	11,725
Horse race	72,223	56,679	18,521	17,745
Horse race (hi grow)	80,866	61,888	21,538	20,938

The first thing we notice is no surprise: these businesses should prefer faster growth to slower (which is not the case in every market). Of course, the problem is that they don't get to choose what the growth rate will be; for the most part, they have to live with what happens.

We could stop at this point. Amalgamated's strategy obviously performs well (in the sense of beating its competitors; we don't know yet if it's the best possible performance), and it performs well regardless of our assumption of market growth. On the other hand, we might be uncomfortable with the wide variation in results for Amalgamated: its performance depends on market growth more than do its competitors' strategies. (Of course, if we know only the numbers above, we should accept the variability in return for the higher overall performance.)

But let's look deeper. Our first question is, with our best-guess for market growth (the original Horse race), does Amalgamated's strategy as well as possible?

If you run a strategy test starting in period 1 (use (F6)), you will see that Raise Q and P does indeed perform the best for Amalgamated (assuming that BigBiz et al. follow the strategies we've assumed for them). So far, so good.

Now let's try running a strategy test for Amalgamated under the other scenarios. To do so, first change the scenario to Horse race (lo grow) — use the (F3) key — then run another strategy test for Amalgamated. Alongside the Raise Q and P strategy you'll see the 56,202 from the table above. You'll also see that that's the best performance for Amalgamated.

Finally, let's run the strategy test under the high-growth version. Change scenarios and run the test and you'll see the 80,866 in the right place. Once again, the best performance.

So, we conclude that Raise Q and P — that is, a premium-quality, premium-pricing strategy — will work best for Amalgamated regardless of the level of market growth. Amalgamated doesn't know what the growth rate will actually be when it makes its strategy selection, but it doesn't matter: assuming its competitors follow the strategies we've simulated, Amalgamated has found its winner.

Notice that we have just determined that Amalgamated need not spend any time or money on research to better predict its market growth (unless, of course, it needs that information for other purposes). Knowing market growth in advance will not change Amalgamated's strategy decision, so why go to the effort of predicting it?[1]

We have not taken into account other aspects of the analysis that we really should. For example, we have assumed that Amalgamated's competitors will not switch their strategies, even though they clearly underperform Amalgamated. In addition, we might want to explore the attractiveness of other strategies because those other strategies might have other characteristics that Amalgamated's management likes. The Raise Q, lag P strategy performs very closely to Raise Q and P, but management might feel more comfortable with its slightly less aggressive pricing.

Nonetheless, we have illustrated how you can begin an analysis with ValueWar to help you see which factors really affect the attractiveness of your strategy. In this case, it seems that market growth does not.

The urge to cut price

One of the most common objectives advocated by managers is to have the lowest price in the market. Underlying this strategy are assumptions about the price sensitivity of customers in the market and about the value of market share as an objective. These assumptions often go unchallenged.

This book is not going to tackle this controversy in general, let alone for any specific business. However, we will show how you could use ValueWar to investigate it for your business.

We will use a methodology similar to the one above in the market-growth test. This time, run ValueWar with the command VW PRICE. This analysis uses three scenarios again: the traditional Horse race, plus a Horse race with low price sensitivity called Horse race (low P) and a Horse race with high price sensitivity called Horse race (hi P). We'll also use the same strategies that we used while testing assumptions about market growth.

---

[1] In the terminology of decision analysis, we have just discovered that market growth has zero value of information in the situation we've assumed.

Here's how cumulative profits looks in period 20:

	Cumulative profits			
	Amalgamated	BigBiz	Consolidated	Diversified
Horse race (low P)	82,281	61,388	16,520	11,783
Horse race	72,223	56,679	18,521	17,745
Horse race (hi P)	56,346	51,958	20,260	21,286

The Horse race line is the same as the one we saw earlier, of course. The other lines show what we might expect: the high-quality strategies followed by Amalgamated and BigBiz do best in markets that aren't price sensitive. We also see that Amalgamated's strategy is more vulnerable than BigBiz's to the assumption about price sensitivity... but that Amalgamated beats BigBiz even if the market is very price sensitive. A manager who selects the Raise Q and P strategy must be careful about his or her forecasts and compensation plan.

Even though we're concentrating on Amalgamated, take a quick look at Consolidated and Diversified. The choice between their strategies — Steady Q, lowest P for Consolidated, and Lowest Q and P for Diversified — *does* depend on the assumption for price sensitivity. If the market is very price sensitive, then Diversified outperforms Consolidated; if it's not, then Consolidated pulls ahead. A management team trying to select between those strategies would find some value (but not much) in getting a more-precise analysis of price sensitivity.

Back to Amalgamated. As we suggested earlier, most managers would be concerned about losing market share, especially by pursuing a high-price strategy (like Amalgamated and BigBiz) in a market that's price sensitive. So, let's take a look at the market-share results.

	Market share (%)			
	Amalgamated	BigBiz	Consolidated	Diversified
Horse race (low P)	33.1	32.4	18.3	16.2
Horse race	28.8	29.3	21.9	20.0
Horse race (hi P)	24.4	25.9	25.6	24.1

It's a toss-up if the market is price sensitive, and a runaway victory for the high-pricers if it's not!

That result seems counterintuitive until you remember that market share is measured as a percentage of dollar sales, not of unit sales. If we look at unit sales, we get a different story.

	Unit share (%)			
	Amalgamated	BigBiz	Consolidated	Diversified
Horse race (low P)	26.3	28.4	24.0	21.3
Horse race	22.1	24.8	27.7	25.4
Horse race (hi P)	18.1	21.1	31.3	29.5

These results show that the performance of Amalgamated's and BigBiz's strategies are, from a unit share perspective, quite dependent on price sensitivity.

The analysis of the three measures — cumulative profits, market share, and unit share — shows that there are two key issues for Amalgamated's management (and for its competitors' as well).

- One: how price sensitive their market is. It makes a big difference in performance.

- The other: what kind of performance really matters to them. Do they value (and reward) profits or share?

In this case, ValueWar has surfaced the issue of measures of success. Amalgamated cannot make a good decision about its tentative strategy without first settling what matters most. If it's profits, then price sensitivity doesn't much matter; cumulative profits are maximized under all three scenarios (though we haven't shown the analyses here) by the Raise Q and P strategy, assuming no change in competitors' strategies. But if it's market share, then other strategies do better... and if it's unit share (or capacity utilization), then Raise Q and P is among the worst performers in a price-sensitive market.

Should be an interesting discussion.

One last observation on this case. Managers segment many markets on the basis of price sensitivity; the analysis we just did could treat the levels of price sensitivity as different segments, not as different assumptions about one market. Managers could then look at the total performance across the segments to see how well a strategy performs across segments.

Building on customer loyalty

Many businesses have little or no data on customer loyalty, switching costs, or any other factor that makes customers want to stay with their current suppliers despite plums offered by the other suppliers. Measuring repeat purchases is *not* the same thing because repeat purchases includes another effect, the current competitiveness of each supplier. Did ABC buy from XYZ because they made another purchase decision (that XYZ won) or because they were loyal to XYZ and didn't even consider switching? The latter is loyalty; repeat purchases combines both.

Note that loyalty doesn't have to be a positive thing, with customers delighted to return time and time again to their suppliers. It can also be born of negative effects such as switching costs, which can make it prohibitively difficult or costly for customers to switch. It can even represent inertia or laziness among customers who buy specific brands out of habit.

We will try a quick analysis with ValueWar to see how loyalty can affect performance. If you run ValueWar with the command VW LOYAL, you can duplicate and expand upon the analyses we're about to show.

We have three scenarios — Horse race (lo loyal), Horse race, and Horse race (hi loyal). The Horse race in the middle is the classic scenario we've used so far. The scenarios differ in that Amalgamated has different levels of customer loyalty: lower than its competitors' in the low-loyalty version, equal to its competitors in the traditional Horse race, and higher than its competitors' in the high-loyalty version.

This time we'll start with the Don't change Q or P strategy for all four businesses. If you look at scenario tests for cumulative profits and market share, this is what you'd see:

	Cumulative profits			
	Amalgamated	BigBiz	Consolidated	Diversified
Horse race (lo loyal)	46,737	65,923	65,923	65,923
Horse race	62,475	62,475	62,475	62,475
Horse race (hi loyal)	75,644	55,955	55,955	55,955

	Market share (%)			
	Amalgamated	BigBiz	Consolidated	Diversified
Horse race (lo loyal)	21.8	26.1	26.1	26.1
Horse race	25.0	25.0	25.0	25.0
Horse race (hi loyal)	29.3	23.6	23.6	23.6

In the Horse race scenario, all the competitors get identical performance because all of them are starting from identical positions and (with the current strategies) none of them is changing its position. In the low-loyalty version, however, the lower loyalty among Amalgamated's customers causes Amalgamated to lose customers simply because they are disproportionately likely to shop around. In the high-loyalty version, Amalgamated keeps more customers than its competitors, so it gradually gains share and, consequentially, profits.

So, even without changing quality or price, Amalgamated's performance depends quite a lot on its level of loyalty. Amalgamated has discovered that it has a large stake in managing its customer loyalty.[1] Important: note that we haven't learned whether Amalgamated needs to

---

[1] In terms of decision analysis, loyalty has a high value of control. Amalgamated can affect its performance if it can manipulate its customers' loyalty.

know its customer loyalty to select a strategy. You can experiment with that analysis; it's similar to the one we began with the market-growth scenarios.

Further analysis shows that loyalty can matter a great deal indeed. Try running the strategies we used for the market-growth and the price-sensitivity analyses above (go to period 1, select new strategies via (F4), and re-run the scenario test). If you use those strategies for the loyalty analysis, you'll see that Amalgamated's cumulative profits are just as sensitive to loyalty as they are to market growth or price sensitivity[1]. In other words, Amalgamated could get as much improvement in performance by improving its customer loyalty (relative to competitors') as it would if its market turned out to have high growth or low price sensitivity.

The money value of time

There's been much talk about time as a competitive weapon: the business that can move fast has an advantage over its poky competitors. You can explore the money value of time with ValueWar.

We've mocked up three scenarios that you can access with the command VW TIME. It's a little different this time; Horse race is first in the list, because it assumes that all competitors can act immediately. In Horse race (med time) and Horse race (hi time), all the competitors except for Amalgamated require increasing amounts of time to make changes in their quality and price.

Using the strategies we've used so far, here's the scenario test displaying cumulative profits:

	Cumulative profits			
	Amalgamated	BigBiz	Consolidated	Diversified
Horse race	72,223	56,679	18,521	17,745
Horse race (med time)	76,291	57,680	30,594	29,086
Horse race (hi time)	79,229	60,195	44,133	41,379

As we expected, we see that Amalgamated's performance goes up as its ability to move faster than its competitors also goes up. In effect, Amalgamated has more of the field to itself: it can stake out its position with less interference from its competitors.

What may be more surprising is that Amalgamated's competitors do better as they get slower. That's because their strategies aren't as good as Amalgamated's (using cumulative profits as our definition of "good"), so anything that slows them down from implementing those strategies actually helps them.

---

[1] Assuming the levels of growth, sensitivity, and loyalty that we've simulated, of course. If we broaden or narrow the range of uncertainty on any of those factors, we will obviously affect which of them have the greatest effect on performance.

So, let's try a different look. What if all the businesses adopted the Raise Q and P strategy? That strategy seems to work well in this market; slowness in implementing it will, presumably, hurt.

	Cumulative profits			
	Amalgamated	BigBiz	Consolidated	Diversified
Horse race	114,595	114,595	114,595	114,595
Horse race (med time)	114,123	108,897	108,897	108,897
Horse race (hi time)	112,715	99,138	99,138	99,138

And indeed it does hurt to be slow in implementing a good strategy. Amalgamated's competitors show that their leisurely pace causes a clear sacrifice in profits. Their slowness even causes Amalgamated to lose just a bit in profits: as you'll see if you display other factors, their slowness in raising prices and quality led them to gain a smidgen of market share at Amalgamated's expense. But it seems that Amalgamated got the better part of that bargain because its competitors spurned a pot of profits for slivers of share.

More ideas and suggestions

We made ValueWar highly interactive so you can analyze many strategy alternatives. Here are some ideas for other analyses.

The low-cost producer

Who is the low-cost producer in a market?

Many businesses aspire to this distinction, but it's not clear a) who it is and b) what it's worth.

Is the low-cost producer the one with the lowest variable costs? Such a business can produce incremental units most cheaply, but if the price of this ability is high fixed costs, then this business will find its cost burden rapidly getting heavier if volume falls. This vulnerability to volume is the curse of capital-intensive industries.

Or is the low-cost producer the one with the lowest fixed costs? This business can most easily withstand a drop in volume, but it has relatively little upside to growth in demand.

You can analyze the difference in these cost structures with ValueWar by manipulating the factors that control fixed and variable costs, costs of capacity, costs of quality, and productivity. You can see what it's like to compete against competitors with cost structure different from your own: they will likely react differently to changes (or expected changes) in volume. You can also explore how your own business's strategic outlook might change if you were to make a change in your cost structure.

Act fast! To knee-jerk or not to knee-jerk?

If you run simulations such as the price war described near the start of this chapter, you'll see how badly knee-jerk reactions can hurt. Businesses that won't let their competitors "get away" with anything may be ruining their own performance. Fully evaluating a strategic move requires both looking more than a few months into the future and taking into account cascading actions and reactions among all the competitors in the market.

You might like to simulate price and quality wars under scenarios other than Horse race. In other scenarios on your ValueWar demo disk, competitors start from non-equal positions and operate in markets with other degrees of quality and price sensitivity. You can see differences in performance under the various scenarios most easily with ValueWar's sensitivity analysis.

Great expectations... will TQM pay off?

Many corporate programs, such as Total Quality Management (TQM), promise major improvements in operations and performance for those companies that take the plunge and implement them wholeheartedly. But many managers fear the brave new world or don't believe that the world ahead will in fact flow with milk and honey.

ValueWar offers a way to simulate the putative effects of TQM or other programs. By specifying appropriate values for factors such as the speed and amount of quality improvements, one-time costs of quality improvements (for process revisions, training, etc.), savings instead of costs for quality improvements, and competitors' likely reactions, you can get a clearer, more-rigorous feel for the benefits of the proposed programs. You can see what has to happen — for example, how much improvement in speed of reaction is required — for the promised advantages to materialize. Moreover, you can test the potential dangers of *not* implementing TQM or other programs while your competitors do.

Are awareness and loyalty campaigns worth the cost?

These questions are similar to the TQM question above, but they involve different ValueWar factors.

Small or young businesses often have awareness problems: they offer terrific products or services, but customers don't know about them. In ValueWar terms, these businesses suffer from low eligibility. The obvious solution is to raise awareness via advertising or other programs.

You can use ValueWar to analyze the cost/benefit properties of these investments. You put in appropriate values for fixed or variable costs (which simulates the cost of an advertising, promotion, or whatever campaign), and you put in appropriate values for the rate of change in eligibility over time. Then you try a second scenario, in which you don't make the investments and you don't get such rapid increases in eligibility. Compare the results (with competitors' likely reactions, of course).

You can analyze loyalty programs in a similar way. Loyalty programs — frequent-flier or -stayer programs, preferred-customer programs, gifts or premiums, and so on — have both costs and benefits that you can simulate with ValueWar. You assess the affects on your fixed and variable costs for the loyalty program, the affects on your perceived quality for having (or not having) those programs, and the likely levels of loyalty that you'd have with or without the programs. This kind of test generally works better than spreadsheet-based assessments that measure costs to the penny while struggling to gauge any competitive advantage of the program at all (or any competitive disadvantage of not having the program).

Incidentally, ValueWar analysis will not necessarily show that awareness, loyalty, or other campaigns will pay off. That's because not all such campaigns do pay off. You want to distinguish those that will from those that won't.

Vertical integration… how much should you control?

Many businesses want to be vertically integrated for the control they get over costs, quality, and the availability of supply. Other businesses shun vertical integration as a diversion from their core competencies or major market focuses.

So, should you vertically integrate or disintegrate? You can use ValueWar to test the alternatives.

By manipulating the factors for fixed and variable costs and the costs and lead times for capacity, you can see the effects of lower or higher vertical integration. Higher vertical integration, for example, will presumably reduce variable costs (because you, not a supplier, pocket the profit) while raising fixed and new-capacity costs (for running a larger operation), possibly lengthening the time it takes to add capacity (because the operations are more complex), and perhaps improving quality (since you'd have more control over the up-stream operations). Then again, you might believe that higher vertical integration carries a risk of reducing quality, on the theory that a specialist can do a better job than a non-specialist. Put in the numbers both ways, run ValueWar, and see whether the probable payoffs exceed the possible risks.

How to improve quality

ValueWar uses a single metric to represent quality, but you can use ValueWar to test different ways to improve (or diminish) quality. The trick is in the numbers you use for the quality-related factors.

When ValueWar simulates an increase-quality strategy, it assesses costs and benefits of the improved quality that depend on the values you supply for factors such as costs (or savings) of changing quality, the time required to change quality, and the amount by which quality can change. If you want to simulate improving quality by using higher-precision, higher-cost components, you'd say that raising quality raises the variable costs of producing the product; if you want to simulate improving quality by investing in higher-precision machinery that will yield lower defect rates, then you'd put in higher fixed costs; if you want to simulate improving quality both ways, you'd put in both costs. In addition, improving quality along multiple dimensions will generally mean a faster rate of change in quality, which you'd specify with another ValueWar factor.

The bottom line is that you can simulate a very wide variety of changes in quality by using the appropriate numbers for the appropriate ValueWar factors.

When to act... it's about timing

It's common practice to draw decision trees to lay out key events ahead. You can run ValueWar simulations to quantify the expected economic value of traversing various branches of the tree.

For example, you could assess the timing of quality or price moves. You could make a move (or even "cheat") now and risk inciting reprisals, or you could wait and see what, if anything, your competitors do.

We simulated a strategy for Diversified in the early chapters of this book that emulated the most profitable business. Essentially a wait-and-see approach, it worked quite well. Note also that waiting may give a blundering competitor a chance to ruin your market, as in the price wars described above.

Another important aspect of timing has to do with competitors' changing preferences. A competitor who has just added capacity will be much less inclined to permit a loss of market share than will one who is running out of existing capacity. Try working with the demo run with the Horse-race scenario: aggressive moves after a competitor has added capacity will cause much more grief than aggressive moves before the competitor adds capacity.

Why they act... smart vs. stupid competitors

Sometimes a competitor behaves badly not because it is stupid but because it is ignorant. Businesses in real life build pre-emptive capacity in part to send a signal to their competitors; if the message doesn't get through, then a competitor may be "stupid" enough to build its own plant.

You could conduct an experiment with managers in your company. Split them into teams and assign them to the various competitors, and have them choose (and revise) strategies two ways, as follows. First, don't allow contact of any kind with the other teams. Second, allow the kind of contact that they'd have from public sources (e.g., from press releases, price lists, and advertisements). Which way do they achieve better performance? What are the implications for managing your own competitors?

Can you afford to wait?

How patient do you expect your company (or your competitors') to be?

Some strategies, particularly those that need lots of up-front investment, take time to pay off. You may choose a strategy that will help your competitors perform well too, so they won't try to clobber you. But if your plan means that they'll have to wait a long time to get their rewards, then they may not cooperate.

The demo run through ValueWar that we covered in Chapters 1 through 5 shows another important aspect of patience. Amalgamated's strategy ultimately performed the best (assuming profit is the key measure of success), but it didn't look like it was going to win for two years. In fact, BigBiz's and Diversified's strategies looked at least equally effective for the first two years. Amalgamated's victory didn't happen because of a change of heart or because of emulating its competitors; it came from steadily following a clear, well-chosen strategy. If Amalgamated had focused solely on its competitors' performance (and not the paths they were following), or if Amalgamated hadn't had the patience to stay the course, it would not have achieved its excellent results.

Do you and they see the same world?

At the start of the demo run, the four competitors were in identical positions, and so they would perceive the world the same way. By the end of a few years, their positions had evolved along different lines, which would make them perceive different worlds.

The competitors had different cost structures, which would give them different preferences in trading off volume against margins. They had different levels of profitability, which would give them different assessments of new opportunities.

Failing to take these differences into account could lead to unintended attacks on each other. For example, since its profits are very volume-sensitive, Consolidated would not like any competitors' action that it would perceive as injurious to its unit sales. Thus, a relatively innocent price cut by Amalgamated (perhaps simply trying to price more like its competitors) could be viewed by Consolidated as a frontal assault. It is for reasons such as these that it's critical to understand the affect on your competitors of the actions you take.

Understanding competitors... why did they do that?

Especially when you're new to ValueWar, you might have a hard time figuring out why a competitor's strategy caused it to make a particular move. That's just like real life! You can see what a competitor did, but you can't know why they did it.

One of the subtler skills you can acquire even from using ValueWar in its demo version is that you can become more astute at understanding why competitors acted (or reacted) the way they did. You will see who did what, and you will learn to infer what made their strategy lead them toward a specific move. You will then become better equipped to predict how they might act (or react) in the future.

If you get *really* good at this kind of role-playing or strategy-inferring, you can even see how several strategies might lead to the same action at one point in time. For example, "Highest Q and P," "Follow success," "Match #1's Q and P," and "Tit for best tat" might all lead a competitor to raise its quality and price in a given period. You will then start considering how those strategies might lead to *different* actions in the future!

Try experimenting with ValueWar to explore questions like these:

- How long must your competitors wait to do well? Must they wait longer than you?
- If your competitors "defect" midway through your plan, can you recover?
- Will another strategy perform well without requiring so much patience from your competitors (or from your Board of Directors)?

Summary

Please remember that the analyses in this chapter are illustrative only. If you or we perform similar analyses for your businesses, we might get similar results... but we might not. Even a factor like customer loyalty could, in some situations, have a negative effect.

How often have you seen market-perceived quality, reaction times, and customer loyalty in strategy reviews? How often do competitors' cost structures appear in reports circulated among managers? How often do strategy-development processes explicitly take competitors' reactions into account or include sensitivity tests to see what uncertainties really affect strategy decisions?

Systems and techniques in common use today, such as financial statements and reports from MIS (management information systems), typically ignore these and other considerations. But now you have seen how often and how much they influence business performance. Part of what's unique about ValueWar — and what makes it valuable as a competitive-strategy tool — is that it does take those factors into account.

STRATEGY ANALYSIS WITH VALUEWAR

VALUEWAR
Reference

Scenario Reference

Using scenarios to test strategies

ValueWar scenarios are comprised of a series of **factors**. The values for these factors control the ValueWar simulations.

For example, one factor is market growth rate. If a scenario has a growth rate of 10%, then market demand will grow at a 10% compound annual growth rate under that scenario.[1] Another scenario might have a -5% growth rate, reflecting a declining market, and so ValueWar would simulate declining demand in that scenario.

The values for the factors have multiple effects. For example, the market growth rate influences capacity additions just as it influences market demand: if the businesses in a market are experiencing steady or diminishing demand, they're unlikely to add new production capacity, while those in rapidly growing markets are almost certain to need capacity additions. The changes in capacity in turn affect fixed costs, and so on.

Thus, by setting appropriate values for ValueWar's factors, ValueWar can be made to realistically simulate markets with totally different characteristics. And, by having multiple scenarios available for analysis (see Chapter 4 of the *Tutorial* section of this book in particular), you can test your strategic options under different assumptions about your market and competitive situation.

Here are just a few examples of different scenarios you can test with ValueWar:

- By manipulating the market growth rate, quality elasticity, and price elasticity factors, you can simulate strategic life under conditions of fast, slow, or expected growth.

- By using different values for quality sensitivity and price sensitivity, you can simulate conditions of customers being more or less sensitive to changes in quality or price; that is, quality-sensitive or price-sensitive markets.

- By specifying various costs (or benefits) for improving quality, you can simulate which methods of improving quality are likely to be most desirable. You can even simulate the consequences of competing against businesses whose ideas of the costs of quality differ from yours. This analysis can demonstrate some fascinating competitive actions and reactions.

---

[1]That growth rate may be further modified by factors that capture elasticity and seasonality effects. You will find details on all these factors in this section of the book.

- By setting the factors for the time it takes for businesses to react to their competitors' actions, you can simulate dealing with fast-moving, aggressive competitors, or slow-moving, complacent competitors, or some of each.

- By controlling the factors for customer loyalty, customer disloyalty, and the time it takes for customers to perceive competitors' changes in quality and price, you can simulate stubborn or inattentive customers (or high switching costs) versus trendy or knowledgeable customers (or low switching costs).

Different competitors Many factors are specified for each business in the simulation. This feature means that you can test the effects of competitors having different capabilities (or liabilities).

Scenarios help you prioritize what to study and know when to change strategy With multiple scenarios at your disposal, you can see whether and when your strategic decisions ought to change. This capability is a major benefit of ValueWar simulations.

For example, if you find that your business's strategy works equally well whether or not the market grows as you expect, then you don't have to worry much about tracking market growth; the rate of growth doesn't change your decisions. On the other hand, if you find that the degree of price sensitivity *does* affect which strategy you should pursue, then you know you should measure price sensitivity carefully and you know that you should consider a shift in strategy if price sensitivity changes over time.

The ValueWar Calibrator

You use the ValueWar Calibrator™ software (not provided with the ValueWar demo) to build your own scenarios. This software lets you enter whatever factor values best model your business's market and competitors.

With the Calibrator, you can create as many scenarios as you like, and change them as often as you like. Thus, the Calibrator lets you quickly and easily update your ValueWar analyses as conditions in your market change or as you encounter opportunities for major changes within your business. For example, you would calibrate new scenarios if:

- Your smallest but most aggressive competitor introduces an unexpected new product with extraordinarily high quality or unusually low price.

- You want to test the potential upside benefits against the possible downside risks of changing your vertical integration (that is, changing how much you make and how much you buy).

- You discover one or more new options for improving the perceived quality of your products and services, and those options have different costs.

- Your market research suggests that your market may be less (or more) price sensitive than you thought.

Factor details

If you want to thoroughly understand ValueWar simulations, or if you want to properly use the ValueWar Calibrator, you need to know how the scenario factors work. That's where this section of *Strategy Analysis with ValueWar* comes in. On the pages that follow you will find the following information about each factor that ValueWar uses or reports in its simulations:

- A definition of the factor.

- What the factor does; that is, how it affects ValueWar simulations.

- A sample value and explanation of the factor.

- "Legal" values for the factor. ("Illegal" values are mathematically meaningless, such as market shares over 100% or below 0%.)

- How to effectively suspend the factor from influencing the simulations, especially if the factor is meaningless for your business.

Most of the factors discussed in this section are entered directly with the Calibrator. Some, however, can be calculated by ValueWar from the entered factors. You don't have to enter those values; ValueWar does the work. For example, you don't have to enter the values for the relative price factor because ValueWar can calculate relative price from the absolute price factor that you do enter.

The factors appear in alphabetical order in this section of the book. Factor names appear in SMALL CAPITALS.

Using factors effectively

As noted above, ValueWar's factors offer enormous analytic richness. By using your imagination and trying various values for the factors, you can explore your business's opportunities, threats, and risks far more realistically, thoroughly, and easily than you could with conventional techniques.

We can add new factors And, of course, we are ready to help you. Let us know if you're having difficulty simulating a particular strategic situation or framing a particular strategic issue. We'll do our best to make suggestions. We can even add new factors to ValueWar if they'd make your analyses work better.

Where to get factor data

You can take advantage of many potential sources of data for scenario factors, especially because you don't need great precision and because (as described above) you can use ValueWar itself to see if you need more precision. Some sources of data are:

- Your own estimates and assumptions.

- Your business's marketing, manufacturing, finance, and sales experts.

- Industry associations, trade journals, or other published data.
- Independent consultants and market researchers.
- ValueWar experts.

You can enter financial data in thousands, millions, etc. as needed. Just be sure to keep your financial data, the size of the market, etc., consistent.

Focusing data on decisions

The data that you enter for ValueWar factors determine the decisions you can explore. You can enter data that focus on relatively small changes, or you can enter more-radical numbers that focus on achieving paradigm-breaking insights.

Don't agonize over factor values! Whether you focus on strategy adjustments or breakthroughs, remember that ValueWar helps you make decisions, not make forecasts with decimal-point precision. For example, the difference between a 5.0% and a 5.2% market growth rate is almost certainly inconsequential *for making strategic decisions*. Therefore, we recommend very strongly that you not delay your analysis if your data are somewhat imprecise.

If you have difficulty obtaining even an estimate of a factor, then try the factor with extreme values and see if it makes a difference in your decisions (use the ValueWar scenario-test feature; see Chapters 4 and 6 in the *Tutorial*). In this way you can use ValueWar to prioritize the competitive information for which you *really* need accuracy. Only if it makes a difference in your decisions should you worry about improving precision.

Factor: ABSOLUTE PRICE

Definition

ABSOLUTE PRICE is the price charged by each business in the ValueWar simulation. It is the actual price that the customer pays after normal discounting, not list price.

This factor is entered for each competitor.

What the factor does

ValueWar uses the ABSOLUTE PRICE from each competitor to calculate RELATIVE PRICEs, and it uses RELATIVE PRICEs (along with several other factors, such as CUSTOMER LOYALTY) to estimate each competitor's market share.

ValueWar also uses ABSOLUTE PRICE to calculate sales for each competitor. Sales equals price times the number of units sold. (Units sold depends on market share, which depends on price.)

If you're simulating a business that offers several products or services, you can use its average price for ABSOLUTE PRICE.

The ABSOLUTE PRICE factor reflects the price charged by each competitor at the start of the ValueWar simulations. The strategies you simulate for each competitor will cause their prices to fluctuate from that point on. ABSOLUTE PRICE will stay within the constraints established by the FEASIBLE CHANGES IN PRICE and FEASIBLE PRICE factors, and it will never go below VARIABLE COSTS.

Sample value

A value of 1,500 means that each unit sold brings in, on average, 1,500 in revenue.

Legal values

Lower limit: 0.01. Upper limit: none.

Suspending the factor

You cannot suspend this factor. You can make ValueWar ignore changes in price by manipulating the DEMAND ELASTICITIES and RESPONSIVENESS TO PRICE factors.

See also

ABSOLUTE QUALITY
DEMAND ELASTICITIES
RELATIVE PRICE
RESPONSIVENESS TO PRICE

Factor: ABSOLUTE QUALITY

Definition

ABSOLUTE QUALITY is the market-perceived quality offered by each business in the ValueWar simulation.

This factor is entered for each competitor.

What the factor does

In ValueWar, ABSOLUTE QUALITY includes *everything* that the customer cares about in making purchase decisions. Thus, quality means not just defects and product/service performance but also purchase criteria such as image, warranties, past interactions, etc. In addition, quality is measured from the *customer's perspective*, not from management's, and it is measured as the *customer's perceptions*, not as some objective "truth."[1]

ValueWar uses the ABSOLUTE QUALITY from each competitor to calculate RELATIVE QUALITY, and it uses RELATIVE QUALITY (along with several other factors, such as CUSTOMER LOYALTY and RELATIVE PRICE) to estimate each competitor's market share.

If you're simulating a business that offers several products or services, you can use its average quality for ABSOLUTE QUALITY.

The ABSOLUTE QUALITY factor reflects the quality offered by each competitor at the start of the ValueWar simulations. The strategies you simulate for each competitor will cause their quality to fluctuate from that point on. ABSOLUTE QUALITY will stay within the constraints established by the FEASIBLE CHANGES IN QUALITY and FEASIBLE QUALITY factors.

Sample value

A value of 75 means that the market perceives the quality of this business's products and services to be at 75 on a scale from 0 (poor) to 100 (excellent).

Legal values

Lower limit: 1. Upper limit: 100.[2]

Suspending the factor

You cannot suspend the effect of this factor. You can make ValueWar ignore changes in quality by manipulating the DEMAND ELASTICITIES and RESPONSIVENESS TO QUALITY factors.

See also

ABSOLUTE PRICE
DEMAND ELASTICITIES
RELATIVE QUALITY
RESPONSIVENESS TO QUALITY

---

[1] Measuring market-perceived quality is an extremely important topic whose scope goes far beyond this book. If you would like to discuss processes for measuring market-perceived quality, please feel free to contact us.
[2] It is possible during ValueWar simulations for ABSOLUTE QUALITY to rise above 100. Please refer to the FEASIBLE QUALITY factor for more detail.

Factor: CAPACITY

Definition

CAPACITY is the number of units of products or services that each business can produce for sale in one period, using the normal number of shifts and normal work rules. It includes capacity made available by sibling businesses in the same corporation.

This factor is calculated for each business from other factors you enter with the ValueWar Calibrator software. Specifically, it is calculated from CAPACITY UTILIZATION and UNIT SALES.

What the factor does

CAPACITY determines the sales capacity of each business in each period. In ValueWar, a business cannot sell more than it can make, and CAPACITY is how much it can make.

The value you enter for CAPACITY reflects the amount of capacity available to each business at the start of the ValueWar simulations.

Businesses can add to CAPACITY in several ways during the simulations. Please refer to the CAPACITY ON ORDER, DEBOTTLENECKING CAPACITY, and ECONOMIC CAPACITY ADDITIONS factors for more details.

Sample value

A value of 2,500 means that the business can produce 2,500 units of products or services in the first period of the simulation.

Legal values

Lower limit: 0. Upper limit: none.

Suspending the factor

ValueWar calculates this factor from other factors you enter. You cannot suspend the effect of this factor. You can prevent changes in CAPACITY by entering appropriate values for other capacity-related factors.

See also

CAPACITY ON ORDER
CAPACITY TRIGGER POINT
CAPACITY UTILIZATION
DEBOTTLENECKING CAPACITY
ECONOMIC CAPACITY ADDITIONS
LEAD TIME TO ADD CAPACITY
MAXIMUM ADDITIONAL CAPACITY
ORDERED CAPACITY READY IN PERIOD

Factor: CAPACITY ON ORDER

Definition

CAPACITY ON ORDER is regular production capacity (if any) that's being built but that's not yet operational.

This factor is entered for each competitor.

What the factor does

This factor controls how much new capacity will be available when construction, hiring, or other arrangements are complete. It is expressed in terms of how many more units may be produced per period.

CAPACITY ON ORDER will come on stream, with its attendant costs, after the number of periods specified by the ORDERED CAPACITY READY IN PERIOD factor. This capacity cannot be canceled or deferred; it will show up as part of CAPACITY, and it will incur costs, even if it is not needed.

The cost of this capacity is controlled by the COST OF CAPACITY factor.

Sample value

A value of 10,000 means that the business will be able to produce 10,000 more units for sale in each period, once the capacity is operational.

Legal values

Lower limit: 0. Upper limit: 10 times current CAPACITY. This factor is entered in the ValueWar Calibrator as a percentage of current CAPACITY (5.0 = 5 times); it is displayed in ValueWar as units of capacity (10,000 = 10,000 units).

Suspending the factor

ValueWar ignores this factor if the ORDERED CAPACITY READY IN PERIOD factor equals -1 (i.e., if no capacity has been ordered).

See also

COST OF CAPACITY
DEBOTTLENECKING CAPACITY
ORDERED CAPACITY READY IN PERIOD

Factor: CAPACITY TRIGGER POINT

Definition

CAPACITY TRIGGER POINT is the level of CAPACITY UTILIZATION at which ValueWar will add capacity (if available). This point may reflect economic considerations or management's preferences about adding capacity.

This factor is entered for each competitor.

What the factor does

CAPACITY TRIGGER POINT controls when ValueWar adds DEBOTTLENECKING CAPACITY or ECONOMIC CAPACITY ADDITIONS for each business.

A high value simulates an unwillingness to add CAPACITY, for whatever reason, unless the business is running near full capacity. High values might be appropriate in cases where CAPACITY is very expensive and it's more sensible to risk turning away some business rather than incur expenses early. This argument might apply even more strongly in highly seasonal markets.

A low value simulates an aversion to being unable to meet customer demand. Low values might be appropriate in cases where CAPACITY is relatively inexpensive or where CUSTOMER LOYALTY is very high. (When CUSTOMER LOYALTY is high, lost customers are hard to regain.)

Sample value

A value of 85% means that a business will add CAPACITY when CAPACITY UTILIZATION reaches 85%.

Legal values

Lower limit: 1%. Upper limit: 200%. Values over 100% mean that ValueWar should not add CAPACITY until customer demand exceeds supply (capacity) for a business's products or services.

Suspending the factor

ValueWar will effectively ignore CAPACITY TRIGGER POINT if no capacity can be added; that is, if DEBOTTLENECKING CAPACITY and MAXIMUM ADDITIONAL CAPACITY both have the value 0.

See also

CAPACITY UTILIZATION
SEASONALITY

Factor:	CAPACITY UTILIZATION

Definition

CAPACITY UTILIZATION is the percentage of CAPACITY that each business is currently employing in order to satisfy its customer demand.

This factor is entered for each competitor.

What the factor does

The CAPACITY UTILIZATION factor indicates the initial position of each business's CAPACITY UTILIZATION. From it and other factors ValueWar calculates data for other factors. For example, ValueWar calculates the initial value for CAPACITY by dividing UNIT SALES by CAPACITY UTILIZATION.

During the simulation — that is, in every period except the initial position — ValueWar calculates CAPACITY UTILIZATION as UNIT SALES divided by CAPACITY.

Each business's CAPACITY UTILIZATION changes over time as it gains or loses unit sales and as it adds new CAPACITY. A business cannot sell more products or services than it is able to produce, so CAPACITY UTILIZATION cannot go over 100%.

Sample value

A value of 85% for CAPACITY UTILIZATION for a business means that it used 85% of its production capacity to make products and services at the start of the simulation.

Legal values

Lower limit: 1%. Upper limit: 100%.

Suspending the factor

You cannot suspend the effect of this factor.

See also

CAPACITY
CAPACITY TRIGGER POINT

Factor:	**COMPETITOR NAMES**

Definition

You can enter names that identify the competitors in the market. ValueWar displays these names on its screens and reports.

What the factor does

COMPETITOR NAMES are the names you see that identify the competitors in the market you're simulating with ValueWar. You can enter a name up to 20 characters long for each competitor.

Sample value

In the Horse-race scenario of the demo version of ValueWar, the COMPETITOR NAMES are "Amalgamated, Inc.," "BigBiz Corporation," "Consolidated Company," and "Diversified Limited."

Legal values

You must supply a COMPETITOR NAME for each competitor. The name must be at least 1 and no more than 20 characters long.

Suspending the factor

You must enter COMPETITOR NAMES. The names you select are used for labeling only; they do not effect ValueWar calculations.

See also

SCENARIO NAME AND DESCRIPTION

Factor:	**COST OF CAPACITY** COST OF DEBOTTLENECKING CAPACITY COST OF REGULAR-CAPACITY ADDITIONS

Definition

COST OF CAPACITY controls the costs incurred for increasing operating capacity. COST OF DEBOTTLENECKING CAPACITY controls the costs of DEBOTTLENECKING CAPACITY, and COST OF REGULAR-CAPACITY ADDITIONS controls the costs of chunks of regular CAPACITY.

These factors are entered for each competitor.

What the factor does

ValueWar adds operating capacity for a business about to hit its CAPACITY TRIGGER POINT, assuming the business is able to add more capacity through debottlenecking and/or regular capacity additions. The COST OF CAPACITY factors control how much the new capacity adds to the business's FIXED COSTS.

If a business adds a chunk of regular CAPACITY, its FIXED COSTS rise by an amount equal to the COST OF REGULAR-CAPACITY ADDITIONS factor. If a business does half of the debottlenecking that it can do, then its FIXED COSTS rise by an amount equal to half the COST OF DEBOTTLENECKING CAPACITY factor.

Sample value

A value of 5,000 for COST OF REGULAR-CAPACITY ADDITIONS means that adding one chunk of regular CAPACITY will make FIXED COSTS go up by 5,000. The 5,000 increase applies to the period in which the new capacity comes on line, and it is applies to every period thereafter.

Legal values

Lower limit: 0.01. Upper limit: none.

Suspending the factor

These factors play no role for businesses that cannot add DEBOTTLE-NECKING CAPACITY or regular CAPACITY.

See also

CAPACITY
DEBOTTLENECKING CAPACITY
ECONOMIC CAPACITY ADDITIONS

Factor: CUMULATIVE PROFITS

Definition

CUMULATIVE PROFITS is the total PROFIT achieved by each business during the ValueWar simulation.

This factor is calculated for each business from revenue and cost factors you enter with the ValueWar Calibrator software.

What the factor does

CUMULATIVE PROFITS starts at 0.0 when the simulation begins and it tracks PROFIT accrued during the simulation. It is generally considered Value-War's primary measure of financial success. It does not drive any other calculations or results in ValueWar.

Sample value

If a business earns PROFIT for the first 5 periods of 2,000, 2,500, 3,000, 4,000, and 4,000, then its CUMULATIVE PROFITS at period 5 will be 15,500.

Legal values

There are no specific limits on this factor. Legal values on its components ensure that this factor will be meaningful.

Suspending the factor

ValueWar calculates this factor from other factors you enter. You cannot suspend the effect of this factor.

See also

PROFIT

Factor: CUMULATIVE SALES

Definition

CUMULATIVE SALES is the approximate total revenue achieved by each business in the market you're simulating with ValueWar prior to the start of the simulation. It grows as SALES grow during the simulation.

This factor is entered for each competitor.

What the factor does

CUMULATIVE SALES tracks SALES accumulated prior to the simulation and accrued during the simulation. It is generally considered a measure of success. It drives the initial value of CUMULATIVE UNIT SALES.

The initial value of CUMULATIVE SALES will generally not be very exact because of imprecision in historical data, market definitions, and so on. Growth in CUMULATIVE SALES will be accurate to the extent of the accuracy in the other factors that drive ValueWar simulations.

This value need not be very exact because CUMULATIVE SALES typically is much larger than SALES in any given period, which makes errors relatively small. The only time you need to be fairly exact on this factor is when a business is relatively young and the EXPERIENCE EFFECT is relatively large ... which is precisely when it's easiest to calculate CUMULATIVE SALES accurately.

Sample value

A value of 100,000 for CUMULATIVE SALES for a business means that it achieved SALES of 100,000 (dollars, pesos, guilder, or whatever) up to and including a given period.

Legal values

Lower limit: 1. Upper limit: none.

Suspending the factor

You cannot suspend the effect of this factor.

See also

CUMULATIVE UNIT SALES
SALES

Factor: CUMULATIVE UNIT SALES

Definition

CUMULATIVE UNIT SALES is the total number of units sold by each business in the market you're simulating with ValueWar prior to the start of the simulation. It grows as UNIT SALES grow during the simulation.

This factor is calculated for each business from other factors you enter with the ValueWar Calibrator software. Specifically, it is calculated from ABSOLUTE PRICE and CUMULATIVE SALES.

What the factor does

CUMULATIVE UNIT SALES drives ValueWar's calculations of the EXPERIENCE EFFECT. Since the EXPERIENCE EFFECT depends on knowing how many doublings of UNIT SALES have occurred, ValueWar needs to know how many units have been sold before the simulation starts.

This value need not be very exact because CUMULATIVE UNIT SALES typically is much larger than UNIT SALES in any given period, which makes errors rather small. The only time you need to be fairly exact on this factor is when a business is relatively young and the EXPERIENCE EFFECT is relatively large ... which is precisely when it's easiest to calculate CUMULATIVE UNIT SALES accurately.

CUMULATIVE UNIT SALES grows over the course of the simulation as each business records additional sales.

Sample value

An initial value of 90,000 for a business means that it had shipped 90,000 units of products or services before the start of the simulation.

Legal values

There are no specific limits on this factor. Legal values on its components ensure that this factor will be meaningful.

Suspending the factor

ValueWar calculates this factor from other factors you enter. You cannot suspend the effect of this factor.

See also

EXPERIENCE EFFECT

Factor: CUSTOMER DISLOYALTY

Definition

CUSTOMER DISLOYALTY indicates the percentage of each business's customers who switch to competitors' products or services even if they "should" remain loyal to the first business.

This factor is entered for each competitor.

What the factor does

CUSTOMER DISLOYALTY simulates the effects of customers who are disloyal because they like to try new products or services. It is the opposite of the CUSTOMER LOYALTY factor. These customers switch to competitors' products or services even if they're sacrificing quality or price as they do so.

In any given period, each business will lose at least the percentage of sales indicated by its CUSTOMER DISLOYALTY percentage. It will be eligible to gain sales that its competitors lose because of their CUSTOMER DISLOYALTY percentages.

Customers with high switching costs would not lightly switch suppliers. Thus, CUSTOMER DISLOYALTY implies customers with low switching costs. CUSTOMER DISLOYALTY can even simulate customers with somewhat inaccurate information about the products and services available to them.

A value of 100% means that a business never keeps a customer it captures. A value of 0% does not mean that a business keeps all the customers it gains; it means only that customers will not make "irrational" decisions to switch to competitors.

Sample value

A value of 20% for a business means that 20% of its previous period's UNIT SALES will go to competitors in the current period, even if its quality and price are the most competitive.

Legal values

Lower limit: 0. Upper limit: 100.

Suspending the factor

A value of 0 for each competitor will make ValueWar simulate a market in which customers stick with businesses whose products and services satisfy them.

See also

CUSTOMER LOYALTY

Factor: CUSTOMER LOYALTY
CUSTOMER LOYALTY
MAXIMUM LOYALTY
MINIMUM LOYALTY

Definition

CUSTOMER LOYALTY indicates the percentage of each business's customers who remain loyal to that business even if they "should" switch to a competitor's products or services. It also captures the effects of switching costs.

CUSTOMER LOYALTY for each competitor can vary only between the limits set by the MAXIMUM LOYALTY and MINIMUM LOYALTY factors. It starts out at the level set by the CUSTOMER LOYALTY factor.

These factors are entered for each competitor.

What the factor does

CUSTOMER LOYALTY simulates the effects of customers who are loyal either by choice or as the result of switching costs. It is the opposite of the CUSTOMER DISLOYALTY factor.

In any given period, each business will make sales to at least the percentage of customers indicated by the CUSTOMER LOYALTY percentage. Another way to look at CUSTOMER LOYALTY is that it shows how many customers are up for grabs in any given period.

CUSTOMER LOYALTY also simulates customers with prohibitively high switching costs because customers with such high switching costs will not jump to a competitor's products or services even if the competitor offers superior quality or price.

A value of 100% means that a business never loses a customer it captures. If all businesses have 100% loyalty, then competition takes place only for new customers entering the market via the MARKET GROWTH RATE factor.

Sample value

A value of 20% for a business means that it will retain 20% of its previous period's UNIT SALES in the current period, even if its quality and price are no longer competitive.[1] It also means that competitors can capture up to 80% of that business's prior UNIT SALES.

Legal values

Lower limit: 0. Upper limit: 100. These limits apply to the initial, MAXIMUM, and MINIMUM LOYALTY factors, subject to the following conditions: 1) MINIMUM LOYALTY must not be greater than MAXIMUM LOYALTY; 2) initial CUSTOMER LOYALTY must not be below MINIMUM LOYALTY; 3) initial CUSTOMER LOYALTY must not be above MAXIMUM LOYALTY.

Suspending the factors

A value of 0 on each of the three factors for each competitor will make ValueWar simulate a market with no loyalty and no switching costs.

---

[1] But if the market shrinks enough, then a business can lose loyal customers.

Scenario Reference

See also   CUSTOMER DISLOYALTY
CUSTOMER LOYALTY GROWTH RATE
EFFECT OF QUALITY ON CUSTOMER LOYALTY

Factor: CUSTOMER LOYALTY GROWTH RATE

Definition

CUSTOMER LOYALTY GROWTH RATE indicates the rate at which loyalty is changing for each competitor in the market.

This factor is entered for each competitor.

What the factor does

CUSTOMER LOYALTY GROWTH RATE simulates the effects on CUSTOMER LOYALTY of programs that change loyalty. For example, investments in frequent-flyer programs can cause loyalty to change over time. The cost of the investments would be captured in FIXED COSTS or VARIABLE COSTS.

CUSTOMER LOYALTY GROWTH RATE may be negative, reflecting decreases in loyalty that might happen in those markets that become more like commodities and focus more on price over time.

Note that estimates of CUSTOMER LOYALTY GROWTH RATE can contain basic and extremely important assumptions about market evolution and customer needs. It may be particularly valuable to test your strategy's sensitivity to the loyalty factors.

Sample value

A value of 5% (0.05) for a business means that its CUSTOMER LOYALTY will increase by 5 percentage points per period, subject to the limits imposed by the MAXIMUM LOYALTY and MINIMUM LOYALTY factors.

Legal values

Lower limit: -1.0. Upper limit: +1.0.

Suspending the factor

A value of 0 for each competitor will make ValueWar simulate a market in which loyalty does not change as a function of time. Loyalty may still change due to changes in quality.

See also

CUSTOMER DISLOYALTY
EFFECT OF QUALITY ON CUSTOMER LOYALTY

Factor: CUSTOMER PERCEPTION TIME
CUSTOMER PERCEPTION TIME... PRICE CHANGES
CUSTOMER PERCEPTION TIME... QUALITY CHANGES

Definition

CUSTOMER PERCEPTION TIME lets ValueWar simulate the time it takes for the market to perceive that one or more businesses have made changes in their quality or price. It also includes the time it takes for customers to act on their new perceptions.

These factors are entered for each competitor.

What the factor does

This factor controls the time lag between the period in which competitors change their quality or price and the period in which customers start to use the new levels of quality or price in their purchase decisions. Thus, CUSTOMER PERCEPTION TIME captures both the time it takes to perceive moves (e.g., the time it takes to inform the market of changes) and the time it takes for the market to act on that information (e.g., the time until sales cycles repeat).

CUSTOMER PERCEPTION TIME also affects the timing of DEMAND ELAS-TICITIES. If the market-average price falls, market growth will be enhanced quickly if CUSTOMER PERCEPTION TIME is immediate, and market growth will be enhanced at a later time if CUSTOMER PERCEPTION TIME imposes a delay.

CUSTOMER PERCEPTION TIME may play an especially important role in seasonal markets. Quality or price changes that are timed to take effect at high-demand times of year should take CUSTOMER PERCEPTION TIME into account.

Sample value

A value of 2 for CUSTOMER PERCEPTION TIME...QUALITY means that customers in this market take 2 periods to perceive and act on changes in a given competitor's quality.

Legal values

Lower limit: 0. Upper limit: 20. These limits apply to both factors.

Suspending the factor

Using a value of 0 for each competitor will make ValueWar essentially ignore these factors. In that case, the market will perceive and react to quality and price changes as soon as those changes occur.

See also

DEMAND ELASTICITIES
SEASONALITY
TIME TO MAKE/PERCEIVE MOVES

Factor: DEBOTTLENECKING CAPACITY

Definition

DEBOTTLENECKING CAPACITY is capacity that's made available as needed by streamlining existing operating processes.

This factor is entered for each competitor.

What the factor does

DEBOTTLENECKING CAPACITY simulates improving the flow of products or services through the slowest or worst-performing operating processes. Improving such flows in effect creates new production CAPACITY because other processes cannot work at their full capacity while they're constrained by the bottlenecks.

If it is available, debottlenecking occurs when capacity utilization reaches 100% or the CAPACITY TRIGGER POINT, whichever is lower. Unlike regular CAPACITY, DEBOTTLENECKING CAPACITY is available immediately; that is, in the period in which it is needed. Also unlike regular CAPACITY, DEBOTTLENECKING CAPACITY can be added in small chunks of as-needed size. However, most businesses have only limited opportunities to add capacity by debottlenecking.

The cost of debottlenecking depends on the COST OF DEBOTTLENECKING CAPACITY factor. Debottlenecking is generally cheaper than adding regular CAPACITY because debottlenecking comes in small chunks).

ValueWar can simulate some of the expected effects of TQM (Total Quality Management) through fairly large amounts of debottlenecking.

Sample value

A value of 20% means that a business can achieve a maximum of 20% more operating CAPACITY through debottlenecking.

Legal values

Lower limit: 0%. Upper limit: 100%.

Suspending the factor

ValueWar ignores the whole concept of debottlenecking if the DEBOTTLENECKING CAPACITY factor has the value 0.

See also

COST OF CAPACITY
MAXIMUM ADDITIONAL CAPACITY

Factor:	**DEMAND ELASTICITIES**
	DEMAND ELASTICITY... PRICE
	DEMAND ELASTICITY... QUALITY

Definition

The two DEMAND ELASTICITIES factors determine to what degree market growth will change if the businesses selling in that market improve (or cut) their ABSOLUTE QUALITY and decrease (or raise) their ABSOLUTE PRICE.

What the factor does

If average quality goes up in a market, market growth will probably go up too, and if average quality falls, growth will probably slacken. If average prices speed up, market growth will probably slow down, and if prices fall, then growth will probably rise.

The DEMAND ELASTICITY: QUALITY and DEMAND ELASTICITY: PRICE factors control how much market growth will change if market-average quality or price changes. The changes in market growth use the MARKET GROWTH RATE factor as a base; that is, they will cause the MARKET GROWTH RATE to rise or fall.

Values for DEMAND ELASTICITY: QUALITY are always positive, meaning that increases in average ABSOLUTE QUALITY make market growth accelerate. Values for DEMAND ELASTICITY: PRICE are always negative, meaning that increases in ABSOLUTE PRICE make market growth (in units) slow down.

ValueWar calculates market-average quality and price as a weighted average of the competitors' ABSOLUTE QUALITY and ABSOLUTE PRICE where the weights are proportional to the competitors' sizes. The averages may be "out of date" if the CUSTOMER PERCEPTION TIME factor says that customers do not immediately perceive changes in quality or price.

Sample value

A value of 5 for DEMAND ELASTICITY: QUALITY means that an increase of 10 points in the market average of ABSOLUTE QUALITY will make market demand grow by 5 percentage points faster than specified by the MARKET GROWTH RATE factor. A value of -12 for DEMAND ELASTICITY: PRICE means that a cut of 10 percent in the market average of ABSOLUTE PRICE will make market demand grow by 12 percentage points faster than specified by the MARKET GROWTH RATE factor.

Legal values

DEMAND ELASTICITY: QUALITY. Lower limit: 0. Upper limit: +100.
DEMAND ELASTICITY: PRICE. Lower limit: -100. Upper limit: 0.

Suspending the factor

If you specify 0 for both these factors, then the market will grow at a steady rate specified by the MARKET GROWTH RATE factor, regardless of what happens to quality and price.

See also

RESPONSIVENESS TO PRICE
RESPONSIVENESS TO QUALITY

Factor: DIFFERENT-ENOUGH PRICE
HIGH-ENOUGH PRICE
LOW-ENOUGH PRICE

Definition

The two DIFFERENT-ENOUGH PRICE factors determine how much higher or lower a business's RELATIVE PRICE has to be for a strategy that seeks a premium-price or discount-price position.

What the factor does

Several ValueWar strategies try to establish a business at a price premium or discount (for example, the HIGHEST Q & P and LOWEST Q & P strategies; see the *Strategy Reference* for details). The DIFFERENT-ENOUGH PRICE factors tell ValueWar how much of a premium or discount is enough.

When a strategy that seeks a price premium is HIGH-ENOUGH PRICE percentage points of RELATIVE PRICE over the second-highest competitor, then the strategy will stop increasing ABSOLUTE PRICE. Note: ValueWar looks for the second-highest competitor that is of sufficient size to be noticed, in accordance with the IGNORE SMALL COMPETITORS factor.

Similarly, when a strategy that seeks a price discount is LOW-ENOUGH PRICE percentage points of RELATIVE PRICE below the second-lowest competitor, then the strategy will stop decreasing ABSOLUTE PRICE. ValueWar looks for the second-lowest competitor that is large enough to be noticed, in accordance with the IGNORE SMALL COMPETITORS factor.

A business seeking a premium (or discount) on RELATIVE PRICE may stop raising (or cutting) price for reasons other than the DIFFERENT-ENOUGH PRICE factors. Specifically, the business might hit limits imposed by the FEASIBLE CHANGE IN PRICE factor.

Sample value

A value of 10% for the HIGH-ENOUGH PRICE factor means that a 10-percentage-point premium in *relative* price is enough; that is, 10% is considered a significant price premium, such that further increases are unwarranted.

Legal values

Lower limit: 0%. Upper limit: 400%. These limits apply to both the HIGH-ENOUGH PRICE and LOW-ENOUGH PRICE factors.

Suspending the factor

If you specify 400%, then ValueWar will essentially ignore these factors. At 400%, an extreme price premium yields a price five times competitors' and an extreme discount means a price one-fifth of competitors'. Since it is extremely unlikely that a business will reach such levels, the DIFFERENT-ENOUGH PRICE factors would not cause competitors to stop raising (or cutting) price.

See also

FEASIBLE CHANGE IN PRICE
MAXIMUM PRICE DISCOUNT
MAXIMUM PRICE PREMIUM

Factor: DIFFERENT-ENOUGH QUALITY
HIGH-ENOUGH QUALITY
LOW-ENOUGH QUALITY

Definition

The two DIFFERENT-ENOUGH QUALITY factors determine how extreme a business's *relative* quality has to be to satisfy the demands of a strategy that seeks premium or "economy" quality.

What the factor does

Several ValueWar strategies try to establish relative quality superiority or inferiority (for example, the HIGHEST Q & P and LOWEST Q & P strategies; see the *Strategy Reference* for details). The DIFFERENT-ENOUGH QUALITY factors tell ValueWar how much higher or lower is enough to fulfill the strategy's intent.

When a strategy that seeks quality superiority is HIGH-ENOUGH QUALITY points of RELATIVE QUALITY over the second-best competitor, then the strategy will stop increasing ABSOLUTE QUALITY. Note: ValueWar looks for the second-best competitor that is large enough to be noticed, in accordance with the IGNORE SMALL COMPETITORS factor.

Similarly, when a strategy that seeks a low-quality position is LOW-ENOUGH QUALITY points of RELATIVE QUALITY below the second-lowest competitor, then the strategy will stop cutting ABSOLUTE QUALITY. ValueWar looks for the second-lowest competitor that is large enough to be noticed, in accordance with the IGNORE SMALL COMPETITORS factor.

A business seeking highest or lowest RELATIVE QUALITY may stop changing quality for reasons other than the DIFFERENT-ENOUGH QUALITY factor. Specifically, the business might hit limits imposed by the FEASIBLE CHANGE IN QUALITY factor.

Sample value

A value of 10 means that a 10-point higher (or lower) position in RELATIVE QUALITY is enough; that is, 10 points is considered a significant quality difference, such that further changes are unwarranted.

Legal values

Lower limit: 0. Upper limit: 100. These limits apply to both the HIGH-ENOUGH QUALITY and LOW-ENOUGH QUALITY factors.

Suspending the factor

If you specify 100, then ValueWar will essentially ignore this factor. It is extremely unlikely that any competitor will ever reach a position of RELATIVE QUALITY that's 100 points above or below its nearest competitor, and therefore the DIFFERENT-ENOUGH QUALITY factors will not cause competitors to stop changing quality.

See also

FEASIBLE CHANGE IN QUALITY
MAXIMUM QUALITY INFERIORITY
MAXIMUM QUALITY PREMIUM

Factor:	ECONOMIC CAPACITY ADDITIONS

Definition

ECONOMIC CAPACITY ADDITIONS is the size of the regular-capacity "chunks" that come on stream when ValueWar adds regular CAPACITY for a business.

This factor is entered for each competitor.

What the factor does

ECONOMIC CAPACITY ADDITIONS controls the amount of new capacity that becomes available each time ValueWar adds ECONOMIC CAPACITY ADDITIONS for a business. It is measured in the number of units of products or services that are added to CAPACITY.

A high value means that it is uneconomical to add regular CAPACITY in small chunks. A small value means that regular CAPACITY can be economically added a small amount at a time.

The cost of ECONOMIC CAPACITY ADDITIONS is controlled by the COST OF REGULAR-CAPACITY ADDITIONS factor. Note that high values of ECONOMIC CAPACITY ADDITIONS may lead to large amounts of fixed costs that will not be covered if demand falls.

Sample value

A value of 150 means that a new chunk of CAPACITY confers the ability to produce an additional 150 units per period.

Legal values

Lower limit: 0. Upper limit: 10. This factor is entered in the ValueWar Calibrator as a percentage of current CAPACITY (5.0 = 5 times); it is displayed in ValueWar as units of capacity (10,000 = 10,000 units).

Suspending the factor

ValueWar will effectively ignore ECONOMIC CAPACITY ADDITIONS if no capacity can be added; that is, if either ECONOMIC CAPACITY ADDITIONS or MAXIMUM ADDITIONAL CAPACITY has the value 0.

See also

CAPACITY
COST OF CAPACITY
FIXED COSTS

Factor: EFFECT OF DECREASING QUALITY ON COSTS
EFFECT OF DECREASING QUALITY ON FIXED COSTS
EFFECT OF DECREASING QUALITY ON VARIABLE COSTS

Definition

The two EFFECT OF DECREASING QUALITY ON COSTS factors define the effects of cutting quality on each business's cost structure. The factors cover effects on FIXED COSTS and on VARIABLE COSTS.

These factors are entered for each competitor.

What the factor does

When businesses diminish their ABSOLUTE QUALITY, they may save money as a result. Their quality cuts can impact costs through any combination of fixed and variable costs.

EFFECT OF DECREASING QUALITY ON FIXED COSTS captures the effect, if any, of cutting quality on fixed expenses. This factor simulates the savings of longer maintenance intervals on equipment, for example, which do not vary with sales volume.

EFFECT OF DECREASING QUALITY ON VARIABLE COSTS captures the effect, if any, of cutting quality on variable expenses. This factor simulates the savings of lower-quality raw materials or components, for example, which vary directly with sales volume.

You can use these factors in any combination to simulate various approaches for decreasing quality. For example, you might use the fixed-cost and the variable-cost factors together to simulate a product-mix shift toward low-precision products.

Both of these factors are expressed as the savings from decreasing ABSOLUTE QUALITY by 10 points. ValueWar assesses pro-rata savings for higher or lower quality cuts; e.g., a 5-point quality cut will save half of what a 10-point cut would save.

ValueWar ensures that costs will not be negative even if changing quality reduces costs.

Important note

You may use negative values for these factors. A negative value means that decreasing quality *increases* the corresponding cost. Thus, a negative value for the variable-cost factor might simulate lower quality resulting from increased reliance on an inefficient, error-prone production process.

Sample value

A value of 5% for EFFECT OF DECREASING QUALITY ON FIXED COSTS means that a 10-point cut in ABSOLUTE QUALITY would reduce FIXED COSTS by 5%, starting in the period in which the decrease in quality occurs.

Legal values

Lower limit: -1000%. Upper limit: +1000%. These limits apply to both the EFFECT OF DECREASING QUALITY ON FIXED COSTS and the EFFECT OF DECREASING QUALITY ON VARIABLE COSTS factors.

Suspending the factor	If you specify 0 for either of these factors, then ValueWar will essentially ignore that factor. The value 0 means that cutting ABSOLUTE QUALITY has no effect on the corresponding (fixed or variable) cost.
See also	EFFECT OF INCREASING QUALITY ON COSTS

Factor: **EFFECT OF INCREASING QUALITY ON COSTS**
EFFECT OF INCREASING QUALITY ON FIXED COSTS
EFFECT OF INCREASING QUALITY ON ONE-TIME COSTS
EFFECT OF INCREASING QUALITY ON VARIABLE COSTS

Definition   The three EFFECT OF INCREASING QUALITY ON COSTS factors define the effects of improving quality on each business's cost structure.

These factors are entered for each competitor.

What the factor does   Businesses may incur costs as they improve their ABSOLUTE QUALITY. Their quality improvements can impact costs through any combination of fixed, variable, and "one-time" costs.

EFFECT OF INCREASING QUALITY ON FIXED COSTS captures the effect, if any, of improving quality on fixed expenses. This factor simulates the costs of higher-precision equipment, for example, which do not vary with sales volume.

EFFECT OF INCREASING QUALITY ON VARIABLE COSTS captures the effect, if any, of improving quality on variable expenses. This factor simulates the costs of better-quality raw materials or components, for example, which vary directly with sales volume.

EFFECT OF INCREASING QUALITY ON ONE-TIME COSTS captures the effect, if any, of improving quality on expenses in one period only. This factor simulates the costs of a training program, a tightly-focused R&D project, or a special advertising campaign, for example, which tend to be relatively transient.

You can use these three factors in any combination. For example, the variable-cost and one-time cost factors can model a change in work rules caused by using better subassemblies.

All three of these factors are expressed as the cost of improving ABSOLUTE QUALITY by 10 points. ValueWar uses pro-rata costs for higher or lower improvements; e.g., a 5-point quality improvement will cost half of what a 10-point improvement would cost.

ValueWar ensures that costs will not be negative even if changing quality reduces costs.

Important note   You may use negative values for any or all of these factors. A negative value means that increasing quality *reduces* the corresponding cost. Thus, a negative value for the variable-cost factor might simulate improving quality by fixing an inefficient, error-prone production process.

You can simulate different competitors' practices in improving quality by using different values for these factors for different competitors. For example, you can see the effects of some competitors' assumptions that quality costs money by using positive numbers for their factors, and the effects of others assuming that quality is free by using negative numbers for their factors.

Sample value

A value of 500 for EFFECT OF IMPROVING QUALITY ON ONE-TIME COSTS means that a 10-point improvement in ABSOLUTE QUALITY would increase FIXED COSTS by 500 in the period in which the improvement occurs.

A value of -5% for EFFECT OF INCREASING QUALITY ON FIXED COSTS means that a 10-point improvement in ABSOLUTE QUALITY would reduce FIXED COSTS by 5%, starting in the period in which the decrease in quality occurs.

Legal values

EFFECT OF IMPROVING QUALITY ON FIXED COSTS. Lower limit: -1000%.
Upper limit: +1000%.
EFFECT OF IMPROVING QUALITY ON VARIABLE COSTS. Lower limit: -1000%.
Upper limit: +1000%.
EFFECT OF IMPROVING QUALITY ON ONE-TIME COSTS. Lower limit: none.
Upper limit: none.

Suspending the factor

If you specify 0 for any of these three factors, then ValueWar will essentially ignore that factor. The value 0 means that improving ABSOLUTE QUALITY has no effect on the corresponding (fixed, variable, or one-time) cost.

See also

EFFECT OF DECREASING QUALITY ON COSTS

Factor: EFFECT OF QUALITY ON CUSTOMER LOYALTY

Definition

EFFECT OF QUALITY ON CUSTOMER LOYALTY indicates the extent to which CUSTOMER LOYALTY changes if ABSOLUTE QUALITY changes.

This factor applies to all competitors in the ValueWar simulation.

What the factor does

EFFECT OF QUALITY ON CUSTOMER LOYALTY simulates the effect that improving (or decreasing) quality has on customers. It lets you simulate the increased loyalty that customers in some markets show to the suppliers who provide them with better and better products and services. It also lets you simulate the way customers lose loyalty for those suppliers who disappoint them with diminished quality.

Since CUSTOMER LOYALTY also serves as a proxy for switching costs, changes in quality may not necessarily affect loyalty. If that's the case in the market you're simulating, use a low or zero value for EFFECT OF QUALITY ON CUSTOMER LOYALTY.

This factor is expressed as the number of percentage points that CUSTOMER LOYALTY will change (up or down) for every 10-point change in ABSOLUTE QUALITY. ValueWar ensures that loyalty will not go beyond the limits set by the MAXIMUM LOYALTY and MINIMUM LOYALTY factors. If CUSTOMER DISLOYALTY is greater than 0, then ValueWar ensures that loyalty will not go below 100% – CUSTOMER DISLOYALTY.

Sample value

A value of 0 means that changes in quality do not affect loyalty. A value of 0.05 means that a 10-point increase (or decrease) in quality results in a 5-percentage-point increase (or decrease) in loyalty.

Legal values

Lower limit: 0. Upper limit: 1.0.

Suspending the factor

A value of 0.0 will make ValueWar simulate a market in which changes in quality do not affect CUSTOMER LOYALTY.

See also

CUSTOMER LOYALTY
CUSTOMER LOYALTY GROWTH RATE

| Factor: | **ELIGIBILITY**
ELIGIBILITY
MAXIMUM ELIGIBILITY
MINIMUM ELIGIBILITY |

Definition

ELIGIBILITY captures the effect of what's called brand recognition or awareness in some industries and approved-vendor lists in others. It also captures the effect of access to distribution channels. Thus, it simulates the extent to which customers consider the businesses eligible suppliers.

ELIGIBILITY for each competitor can vary only between the limits set by the MAXIMUM ELIGIBILITY and MINIMUM ELIGIBILITY factors. It starts out at the level set by the ELIGIBILITY factor.

These factors are entered for each competitor.

What the factor does

Customers will not buy from businesses they don't consider "eligible." Thus, ELIGIBILITY lets ValueWar simulate how some businesses have difficulty making sales because customers are not aware of them (or do not yet trust them), while others do not suffer from these constraints.

The ELIGIBILITY factor sets the values for each business's ELIGIBILITY at the start of the simulation. Thereafter, ELIGIBILITY can change over time as a function of other eligibility-related factors. ELIGIBILITY will stay between the limits set by the MAXIMUM ELIGIBILITY and MINIMUM ELIGIBILITY factors.

If a business has 0% ELIGIBILITY, no one will buy from it. If it has 100% ELIGIBILITY, the entire market will consider buying from it; whether such a business actually makes any sales will depend on its RELATIVE QUALITY, RELATIVE PRICE, ability to satisfy demand (CAPACITY), and so on.

Sample value

A value of 60% means that this business competes for 60% of the market's UNIT SALES. Conversely, 40% of the market's UNIT SALES are in effect closed off to this business no matter how attractive its RELATIVE QUALITY or RELATIVE PRICE. Thus, 60% ELIGIBILITY means that a business's MARKET SHARE will be 60% of what it would have gotten, given its RELATIVE QUALITY, RELATIVE PRICE, and so on, if it had had 100% ELIGIBILITY.

Legal values

Lower limit: 0%. Upper limit: 100%. These limits apply to the initial, MAXIMUM, and MINIMUM ELIGIBILITY factors, subject to the following conditions: 1) MINIMUM ELIGIBILITY must not be greater than MAXIMUM ELIGIBILITY; 2) initial ELIGIBILITY must not be below MINIMUM ELIGIBILITY; 3) initial ELIGIBILITY must not be above MAXIMUM ELIGIBILITY.

Suspending the factors

If you enter 100% for all three ELIGIBILITY factors, then ValueWar will effectively ignore the ELIGIBILITY concept. (In addition, ValueWar will ignore the change-in-eligibility factors if these three are all set to 100%.) All businesses will be eligible to sell to the whole market.

See also

ELIGIBILITY CHANGES WITH SHARE CHANGES
ELIGIBILITY GROWTH RATE

Factor: ELIGIBILITY CHANGES WITH SHARE CHANGES
ELIGIBILITY DECREASES WITH SHARE DECREASES
ELIGIBILITY INCREASES WITH SHARE INCREASES

Definition

ELIGIBILITY can change as market share changes. ValueWar provides the ELIGIBILITY CHANGES WITH SHARE CHANGES factors to simulate those changes in ELIGIBILITY.

What the factor does

As share increases, businesses gain credibility and awareness; as share falls, businesses lose credibility or become unfashionable.

The ELIGIBILITY INCREASES WITH SHARE INCREASES factor captures the gaining-credibility and increasing-awareness effects. The ELIGIBILITY DECREASES WITH SHARE DECREASES factor captures the losing-credibility and becoming-unfashionable effects.

Both factors are measured in terms of the number of percentage points that ELIGIBILITY changes for each point of increase or decrease in MARKET SHARE. ValueWar applies the ELIGIBILITY INCREASES WITH SHARE INCREASES factor when MARKET SHARE grows, and the ELIGIBILITY DECREASES WITH SHARE DECREASES factor when MARKET SHARE falls. By having two factors, you can simulate different rates of change in ELIGIBILITY for share increases and decreases.

Sample value

A value of 5 for ELIGIBILITY INCREASES WITH SHARE INCREASES means that each business's ELIGIBILITY grows by 5 percentage points for each percentage point of MARKET SHARE it gains.

Legal values

Lower limit: 0. Upper limit: 100. These limits apply to both factors.

Suspending the factor

If you enter 0 for ELIGIBILITY INCREASES (or DECREASES) WITH SHARE INCREASES (or DECREASES), then these factors are suspended and ELIGIBILITY will not change as MARKET SHARE increases or decreases, respectively.

See also

ELIGIBILITY
ELIGIBILITY GROWTH RATE

Factor: ELIGIBILITY GROWTH RATE

Definition

ELIGIBILITY can change over time. ValueWar provides the ELIGIBILITY GROWTH RATE factor to simulate such changes.

What the factor does

ELIGIBILITY measures, in part, awareness of a business's products and services. Market awareness of those products and services tends to rise over time, perhaps but not necessarily as a result of advertising or other investments, and so ValueWar provides a mechanism to simulate businesses' increasing ability to sell to the whole market.

This factor is measured in terms of the number of percentage points that ELIGIBILITY rises in each period. A value of 0 means that ELIGIBILITY does not change as a function of time. Positive numbers mean that ELIGIBILITY grows over time; negative numbers mean that ELIGIBILITY falls over time.

The net change to each business's ELIGIBILITY depends on the ELIGIBILITY CHANGES WITH SHARE CHANGES factors, along with its market-share changes, as well as the ELIGIBILITY GROWTH RATE. Changes to ELIGIBILITY will not exceed the bounds set by the MAXIMUM ELIGIBILITY and MINIMUM ELIGIBILITY factors.

Sample value

A value of 5 for ELIGIBILITY GROWTH RATE means that each business's ELIGIBILITY grows by 5 percentage points in each period.

Legal values

Lower limit: -99. Upper limit: 100.

Suspending the factor

If you enter 0 for the ELIGIBILITY GROWTH RATE, then ELIGIBILITY will not change as a function of time.

See also

ELIGIBILITY
ELIGIBILITY CHANGES WITH SHARE CHANGES

| **Factor:** | **EXPERIENCE EFFECT** |

Definition

EXPERIENCE EFFECT captures the degree to which businesses acquire knowledge, equipment, and expertise that reduce their variable operating costs over time.

This factor is entered for each competitor.

What the factor does

EXPERIENCE EFFECT controls the rate of reduction in VARIABLE COSTS that businesses can enjoy as their cumulative production volume grows. It is measured as the percentage of VARIABLE COSTS that remain after each doubling of accumulated unit production.

This factor also simulates the benefits of going down a "learning curve."

A high number for the EXPERIENCE EFFECT — i.e., a value near 1.0 — has little effect on costs since it means a large percentage of VARIABLE COSTS remain as production grows. Low numbers express an assumption that costs will decline at a more-rapid rate.

The expected reductions in costs caused by the EXPERIENCE EFFECT (and the learning curve) are often used as a rationale for aggressively seeking increases in (unit) market share. However, when selecting a value for this factor it is important to remember that these reductions in cost are not automatic. They require active management and employees.

Sample value

A value of 95% means that VARIABLE COSTS will decline by 5% (that is, 95% of the costs will remain) after a doubling in cumulative unit production.

Legal values

Lower limit: 1%. Upper limit: 100%.

Suspending the factor

ValueWar will simulate no EXPERIENCE EFFECT if the factor is set to 100%, which means that costs don't change — i.e., 100% of costs remain — even after cumulative unit production doubles.

See also

PRODUCTIVITY

Factor: **FEASIBLE CHANGES IN PRICE**
FEASIBLE DECREASES IN PRICE
FEASIBLE INCREASES IN PRICE

Definition

The two FEASIBLE CHANGES IN PRICE factors — decrease and increase — set the limits on each business's ability to change ABSOLUTE PRICE.

These factors are entered for each competitor.

What the factor does

The two FEASIBLE CHANGES IN PRICE factors control the rate at which each business increases or decreases its ABSOLUTE PRICE. These constraints on change may reflect market sensitivities, management preferences, or any other limiting factor.

ValueWar strategies (see the *Strategy Reference* part of the *Reference* section) usually call for changes in ABSOLUTE PRICE. The FEASIBLE CHANGES IN PRICE factors determine how much a business's ABSOLUTE PRICE will change when its strategy calls for a change. The change in price may be less than the feasible amount if a smaller change is "enough," as controlled by the DIFFERENT-ENOUGH PRICE factors.

Changes in price are measured in the number of percentage points of ABSOLUTE PRICE that a business can move up or down in one period.

Sample value

Values of 5% and 10% for the decrease and increase FEASIBLE CHANGES IN PRICE will cause a business to cut its ABSOLUTE PRICE by 5% in each period that it makes a cut, and to increase its ABSOLUTE PRICE by 10% in each period that it makes an increase.

Legal values

Lower limit: 0%. Upper limit: 100%. These limits apply to both the FEASIBLE DECREASES IN PRICE and FEASIBLE INCREASES IN PRICE factors.

Suspending the factor

You cannot suspend the effects of these factors.

See also

ABSOLUTE PRICE
DIFFERENT-ENOUGH PRICE
FEASIBLE PRICE

Factor:	**FEASIBLE CHANGES IN QUALITY**
	FEASIBLE DECREASES IN QUALITY
	FEASIBLE INCREASES IN QUALITY

Definition

The two FEASIBLE CHANGES IN QUALITY factors — decrease and increase — set the limits on each business's ability to change ABSOLUTE QUALITY.

These factors are entered for each competitor.

What the factor does

The two FEASIBLE CHANGES IN QUALITY factors control the rate at which each business increases or decreases its ABSOLUTE QUALITY. These constraints on change may reflect technological limits, management preferences, or any other limiting factor.

ValueWar strategies (see the *Strategy Reference* part of the *Reference* section) usually call for changes in ABSOLUTE QUALITY. The FEASIBLE CHANGES IN QUALITY factors determine how much a business's ABSOLUTE QUALITY will change when its strategy calls for a change. The change in quality may be less than the feasible amount if a smaller change is "enough," as controlled by the DIFFERENT-ENOUGH QUALITY factors.

Changes in quality are measured in the number of points of ABSOLUTE QUALITY that a business can move up or down in one period.

Sample value

Values of 5 and 10 for the decrease and increase FEASIBLE CHANGES IN QUALITY will cause a business to cut its ABSOLUTE QUALITY by 5 points in each period that it makes a cut, and to increase its ABSOLUTE QUALITY by 10 points in each period that it makes an increase.

Legal values

Lower limit: 0. Upper limit: 100. These limits apply to both the FEASIBLE DECREASES IN QUALITY and the FEASIBLE INCREASES IN QUALITY factors.

Suspending the factor

You cannot suspend the effects of these factors.

See also

ABSOLUTE QUALITY
DIFFERENT-ENOUGH QUALITY
FEASIBLE QUALITY

Factor:	**FEASIBLE PRICE**
	MAXIMUM FEASIBLE PRICE
	MINIMUM FEASIBLE PRICE
	MINIMUM PRICE (% OF VARIABLE COSTS)

Definition

The minimum and maximum FEASIBLE PRICE factors set the outer limits on each business's ability to change ABSOLUTE PRICE.

These factors are entered for each competitor.

What the factor does

FEASIBLE PRICE controls the extent to which each business can change its ABSOLUTE PRICE. The price limits may reflect market constraints, management preferences, or any other limiting factor.

ValueWar strategies (see the *Strategy Reference* part of the *Reference* section) usually call for changes in ABSOLUTE PRICE. The FEASIBLE PRICE factors set boundaries beyond which the strategies may not go.

Another limiting factor is MINIMUM PRICE (% OF VARIABLE COSTS): ValueWar will not allow unit prices to fall below some percentage of variable costs per unit, even if such a price is within the FEASIBLE PRICE constraints. Example: if the percentage is 110%, then unit price must stay at least 10% above variable costs per unit. If the percentage is 95%, then price can dip 5% below variable costs.

The minimum and maximum FEASIBLE PRICE factors override the MINIMUM PRICE (% OF VARIABLE COSTS) factor: prices may not go below the minimum FEASIBLE PRICE, even if a price that low would satisfy the MINIMUM PRICE (% OF VARIABLE COSTS) constraint.

Sample value

Values of 5,000 and 10,000 for the minimum and maximum FEASIBLE PRICE will prevent a business's ABSOLUTE PRICE from moving below 5,000 or above 10,000. A value of 1.00 (100%) for MINIMUM PRICE (% OF VARIABLE COSTS) means that price may not go below variable costs.

Legal values

Lower limit: 0.1. Upper limit: none. These limits apply to both the MAXIMUM and MINIMUM FEASIBLE PRICE factors.

MINIMUM PRICE (% OF VARIABLE COSTS): lower limit: 0.01. Upper limit: none.

Suspending the factor

ValueWar requires limits to changes in price. You can simulate the least-restrictive limits to changes in price by setting the FEASIBLE PRICE and MINIMUM PRICE (% OF VARIABLE COSTS) factors to extreme values.

See also

ABSOLUTE PRICE
FEASIBLE QUALITY

Factor: FEASIBLE QUALITY
MAXIMUM FEASIBLE QUALITY
MINIMUM FEASIBLE QUALITY

Definition

The minimum and maximum FEASIBLE QUALITY factors set the outer limits on each business's ability to change ABSOLUTE QUALITY.

These factors are entered for each competitor.

What the factor does

FEASIBLE QUALITY controls the extent to which each business can change its ABSOLUTE QUALITY. The quality limits may reflect technological constraints, management preferences, or any other limiting factor.

ValueWar strategies (see the *Strategy Reference* part of the *Reference* section) usually call for changes in ABSOLUTE QUALITY. The FEASIBLE QUALITY factors set boundaries beyond which the strategies may not go.

Sample value

Values of 40 and 70 for the minimum and maximum FEASIBLE QUALITY will prevent a business's ABSOLUTE QUALITY from moving below 40 or above 70.

Legal values

MINIMUM FEASIBLE QUALITY: lower limit: 1. Upper limit: 100.
MAXIMUM FEASIBLE QUALITY: lower limit: 1. Upper limit: 150.[1]
The maximum should be higher than the minimum.

Suspending the factor

ValueWar requires limits to changes in quality. You can simulate the least-restrictive limits to changes in quality by setting the FEASIBLE QUALITY factors at their limits.

See also

ABSOLUTE QUALITY
FEASIBLE PRICE

---

[1] The upper limit on MAXIMUM FEASIBLE QUALITY reflects the possibility that ABSOLUTE QUALITY can, under certain circumstances, rise over 100. This extreme value would simulate, in effect, changes in customer assessments of quality. An equivalent but more-difficult way to simulate these changes would be to scale downward all data on ABSOLUTE QUALITY to show that customer expectations have risen, and so perceived quality has fallen.

Factor: **FIRST POSSIBLE MOVE**
FIRST POSSIBLE PRICE MOVE
FIRST POSSIBLE QUALITY MOVE

Definition

The FIRST POSSIBLE MOVE factors let ValueWar simulate situations in which businesses cannot immediately change quality and/or price.

Both factors are entered for each competitor.

What the factor does

These factors control at what time each competitor can make its first quality or price move. ValueWar uses these factors to simulate the effects of known delays, complacency/inertia, physical limits to action, product-launch schedules, and so on.

The FIRST POSSIBLE MOVE factors are measured in periods. Thus, a value of 5 for FIRST POSSIBLE PRICE MOVE means that that competitor cannot change its price until period 5 at the earliest.

ValueWar makes the following exceptions to these time delays: 1) non-strategy moves override these factors, thereby allowing quality and/or price changes before the first period for a move has been reached; 2) quality or price moves may occur that are forced by the MAXIMUM PRICE DIFFERENCE and MAXIMUM QUALITY DIFFERENCE factors, even if those moves violate these time delays.

Note that the FIRST POSSIBLE MOVE factors indicate the earliest time that a move may occur (subject to the exceptions mentioned above). If a business also has a time delay due to the TIME TO MAKE/PERCEIVE MOVES factors, then the first action will not show up until after both delays.

As a convenience, you can specify the special value -1 for the FIRST POSSIBLE PRICE MOVE factor. The -1 value means that the first time that a price move can occur will be the first period that a quality move can occur. Thus, if you want to change the first time that quality and price moves can occur, you only have to change one value — the one for the FIRST POSSIBLE QUALITY MOVE factor — to effectively reset both.

Sample value

A value of 1 means that quality or price action can occur from the start of the simulation (depending also on other factors). Note that a value of 1 does not require action in period 1; it merely indicates that action is possible in period 1. Whether a business actually moves will depend on its strategy, its competitors, its TIME TO MAKE/PERCEIVE MOVES, and so on.

Legal values

Lower limit: 1. Upper limit: 20. These limits apply to both factors, except that FIRST POSSIBLE PRICE MOVE also accepts the special value of -1 to say that price moves can start in the same period as quality moves.

Suspending the factor

If you specify 1 for all competitors, then ValueWar will essentially ignore these factors. All competitors will make moves as soon as they wish.

See also

CUSTOMER PERCEPTION TIME
TIME BETWEEN MOVES
TIME TO MAKE/PERCEIVE MOVES

Factor: FIXED COSTS

Definition

FIXED COSTS are all costs incurred as a normal part of doing business and that do not vary with unit sales or production volume.

This factor is entered for each competitor.

What the factor does

FIXED COSTS describes part of each business's cost structure for ValueWar. It includes such non-volume-dependent expenses as advertising, depreciation, R&D, marketing, and accounting staffs, and so on.

ValueWar uses FIXED COSTS in part to simulate the costs of additional CAPACITY. If CAPACITY doubles, for example, FIXED COSTS will double. This relationship captures the fact that capacity additions are generally correlated with expansions in other aspects of a business. In other words, a business that's adding operating CAPACITY is likely to expand its scope or scale in other areas as well.

Along with the VARIABLE COSTS factor, FIXED COSTS sets the initial value for each business's cost structure at the start of the ValueWar simulations. FIXED COSTS can change over time as a result of PRODUCTIVITY and as a result of changes in CAPACITY and QUALITY.

The nature of a business's cost structure — that is, its mix of fixed and variable costs, and the amount of each — is crucial not only to its financial performance but also to understanding its strategic motives. For example, a business with relatively high FIXED COSTS will be very sensitive to sales volume and SEASONALITY, whereas a business with relatively high VARIABLE COSTS will be more sensitive to prices. You can use ValueWar to see how changes in quality and price can affect your competitors in ways substantially different from their effects on your business.

Sample value

A value of 7,000 for a business means that its FIXED COSTS start at 7,000 when the simulation begins.

Legal values

Lower limit: 0. Upper limit: none.

Suspending the factor

You cannot suspend the effect of this factor.

See also

DEBOTTLENECKING CAPACITY
EFFECT OF DECREASING QUALITY ON COSTS
EFFECT OF INCREASING QUALITY ON COSTS
ECONOMIC CAPACITY ADDITIONS
PRODUCTIVITY
VARIABLE COSTS

Factor: IGNORE SMALL COMPETITORS

Definition

IGNORE SMALL COMPETITORS lets ValueWar simulate the behavior of large businesses who ignore the actions of small competitors despite the small businesses being acutely aware of the actions of their large competitors.

This factor is entered for each competitor.

What the factor does

Various ValueWar strategies cause businesses to examine the behavior of their competitors before making changes to quality or price (see the *Strategy Reference* in the *Reference* section of this book). ValueWar uses the IGNORE SMALL COMPETITORS factor to determine which competitors' behavior gets examined.

A high value of this factor for a business means that it will only take into account the actions of its largest competitors. A value of 100% means that the business will ignore the actions of all its competitors.

A low value of this factor for a business means that it will take into account the actions of most or all of its competitors. A value of 0% means that the business will observe the actions of all its competitors.

You could use this factor in a supermarket market, for example, to simulate large chains watching each other closely but essentially ignoring the behavior of smaller, local merchants. (You can even use this factor to make ValueWar simulate markets with only two or three competitors instead of the usual four. You'd define one or two tiny competitors and then use the IGNORE SMALL COMPETITORS factor to make the "real" competitors ignore the tiny ones.)

If a competitor is above the "ignoring threshold" in any given period, its actions will be taken into account in that period. If the same competitor is below the threshold in other periods, its actions will be ignored in those periods.

Sample value

A value of 25% for a business means that it will ignore the actions of any competitor with less than 25% market share.

Legal values

Lower limit: 0%. Upper limit: 100%.

Suspending the factor

You can specify a market in which all competitors watch all other competitors by specifying a value of 0% for each competitor.

See also

MARKET SHARE

Factor: LEAD TIME TO ADD CAPACITY

Definition   LEAD TIME TO ADD CAPACITY is the time it takes to order new regular CAPACITY and to bring it on stream.

This factor is entered for each competitor.

What the factor does   LEAD TIME TO ADD CAPACITY controls the time it takes for each business to obtain new regular CAPACITY. It is measured in periods (that is, quarters). If, for example, it takes 8 periods (2 years) to obtain new capacity and the business runs out of capacity after 6 periods, then the business will have to turn away customers for 2 periods while it waits for the new capacity.

A high value means that it is uneconomical to add regular CAPACITY in small chunks. A small value means that regular CAPACITY can be economically added a small amount at a time.

Sample value   A value of 8 means that a new chunk of regular CAPACITY takes 8 periods (2 years) to build.

Legal values   Lower limit: 0. Upper limit: 20.

Suspending the factor   ValueWar will effectively ignore LEAD TIME TO ADD CAPACITY if no capacity can be added; that is, if MAXIMUM ADDITIONAL CAPACITY has the value 0.

See also   CAPACITY

Factor: MARKET CYCLES

Definition

MARKET CYCLES let you describe business or economic cycles. Each cycle covers key information about market growth, price sensitivity, and quality sensitivity, as well as the duration of the cycle.

You can specify up to five cycles.

What the factor does

MARKET CYCLES control the basic characteristics of the market you're simulating with ValueWar. For each cycle you specify, you enter up to four numbers:

1) The period at which the cycle ends.

2) The MARKET GROWTH RATE for the cycle.

3) Customers' RESPONSIVENESS TO PRICE for the cycle.

4) Customers' RESPONSIVENESS TO QUALITY for the cycle.

You enter five MARKET CYCLES. Enter -1 for the ending period if you can express the desired growth rates and cycles in fewer than five cycles. If ValueWar encounters -1 for an ending period, it ignores other information, if any, about that cycle.

If you are using the ValueWar Calibrator software, you have a copy of a sample scenario-information file. That file shows how to enter the data for MARKET CYCLES.

Sample value

A value of 10 for the ending period of a cycle indicates that the associated information about the cycle (market growth and sensitivity to quality and price) pertains to a cycle that ends in period 10.

Legal values

The data for MARKET GROWTH RATE, RESPONSIVENESS TO PRICE, and RESPONSIVENESS TO QUALITY must all be legal, as specified by the descriptions of those factors elsewhere in this book. The ending period for each cycle must be between the lower limit of 1 and the upper limit of 20. Special value: -1. At least one of the five ending periods for the MARKET CYCLES must have a value of 20 for the ending period. The cycles must be in ascending order of ending periods (except for -1's, which can be interspersed as desired).

Suspending the factor

You cannot suspend the effect of this factor.

See also

MARKET GROWTH RATE
RESPONSIVENESS TO PRICE
RESPONSIVENESS TO QUALITY

Factor: MARKET GROWTH RATE

Definition
MARKET GROWTH RATE is the compound annual growth rate (CAGR) of the market you are simulating with ValueWar. It is measured as the growth rate of unit sales; that is, it is "real" growth, unaffected by inflation.

You can enter up to five growth rates, which lets you simulate business and economic cycles. See the factor description for MARKET CYCLES for more details.

What the factor does
MARKET GROWTH RATE controls the basic growth of the market you're simulating with ValueWar.

Other ValueWar factors — specifically, SEASONALITY and DEMAND ELASTICITIES for quality and price — modify the basic growth rate. For example, if the average price charged in the market goes down, then the unit sales in the market will grow somewhat faster than the base MARKET GROWTH RATE.

ValueWar applies the MARKET GROWTH RATE to the SIZE OF MARKET that starts the simulation. In each subsequent period, it applies the MARKET GROWTH RATE plus whatever adjustments are appropriate as determined by SEASONALITY and DEMAND ELASTICITIES.

Sample value
A value of 6% means that market demand for units of products and services will grow at a 6% CAGR, all else being equal. In other words, market demand in one period will be 6% higher than demand four periods earlier. SEASONALITY and changes in market-average quality or price may yield higher or lower growth rates, as mentioned above.

Legal values
Lower limit: -100%. Upper limit: +100%.

Suspending the factor
You cannot suspend the effect of this factor.

See also
DEMAND ELASTICITIES
MARKET CYCLES
SEASONALITY
SIZE OF MARKET

Factor: MARKET SHARE

Definition

MARKET SHARE is the percentage of customer purchases captured by each competitor, where purchases are measured in SALES, not units.

This factor is calculated for each business from other factors you enter with the ValueWar Calibrator software. Specifically, it is calculated from ABSOLUTE PRICE, SIZE OF MARKET, and UNIT SHARE.

What the factor does

MARKET SHARE indicates the relative size of each business in the simulation, with "size" measured in SALES.

Changes in MARKET SHARE during the ValueWar simulation are driven primarily by RELATIVE QUALITY and RELATIVE PRICE. The extent to which those factors determine MARKET SHARE is controlled by the RESPONSIVENESS TO QUALITY and PRICE factors. RELATIVE QUALITY and RELATIVE PRICE are determined by ABSOLUTE QUALITY and ABSOLUTE PRICE, which are controlled by the market strategies you select for the competitors in the simulation.

ValueWar refines its estimates of MARKET SHARE by applying factors such as CAPACITY, CUSTOMER LOYALTY, CUSTOMER DISLOYALTY, CUSTOMER PERCEPTION TIMES, ELIGIBILITY, and so on. By combining these factors with its emphasis on measuring quality and price relative to competitors', ValueWar achieves a high degree of realism in its market-share projections.

Sample value

A value of 20% for a business in a given period means that it accounted for 20% of the SALES in the market in that period.

Legal values

Lower limit: 1%. Upper limit: 100%.

Suspending the factor

ValueWar calculates this factor from other factors you enter. You cannot suspend the effect of this factor.

See also

UNIT SHARE

Factor: MAXIMUM ADDITIONAL CAPACITY

Definition

MAXIMUM ADDITIONAL CAPACITY is the maximum total amount of new regular CAPACITY that a business can add. The maximum may reflect physical limitations or limits to management's willingness to add CAPACITY. It does not include CAPACITY ON ORDER.

This factor is entered for each competitor.

What the factor does

MAXIMUM ADDITIONAL CAPACITY controls how much CAPACITY ValueWar can add for each competitor that needs to add capacity to satisfy customer demand. Competitors cannot sell what they cannot produce, so MAXIMUM ADDITIONAL CAPACITY may represent limits to competitors' abilities to grow.

MAXIMUM ADDITIONAL CAPACITY does not include capacity added from debottlenecking; it covers only regular CAPACITY, which is added in chunks whose size is determined by ECONOMIC CAPACITY ADDITIONS. The total amount of new CAPACITY that ValueWar can add equals MAXIMUM ADDITIONAL CAPACITY plus DEBOTTLENECKING CAPACITY.

Sample value

A value of 50% means that a business can achieve a maximum of 50% more regular operating capacity. If DEBOTTLENECKING CAPACITY equals 20%, then ValueWar will add a maximum of 20% new capacity through debottlenecking (first) and then up to 50% more capacity through regular capacity additions (next), for a total of 70% more capacity.

Legal values

Lower limit: 0%. Upper limit: none.

Suspending the factor

ValueWar will not add regular CAPACITY for any competitor whose MAXIMUM ADDITIONAL CAPACITY factor has the value 0.

See also

CAPACITY
CAPACITY ON ORDER
CAPACITY TRIGGER POINT
COST OF CAPACITY
DEBOTTLENECKING CAPACITY
ECONOMIC CAPACITY ADDITIONS

Factor: MAXIMUM PRICE DIFFERENCE
MAXIMUM PRICE DISCOUNT
MAXIMUM PRICE PREMIUM

Definition

The MAXIMUM PRICE DIFFERENCE factors determine how much higher or lower a business's price can be (relative to its competitors') before its price becomes strategically unacceptable.

What the factor does

A business's RELATIVE PRICE changes due to its and its competitors' pricing actions. The resulting intended or inadvertent change in RELATIVE PRICE may make the business's price so high that it's no longer competitive, or the business's price may go so low that the business foregoes profits for no real competitive benefit.

A real business wouldn't let its price rise so high that it becomes uncompetitively expensive. ValueWar uses the MAXIMUM PRICE PREMIUM factor to prevent a business from pricing itself out of its market. This factor may override a business's strategy: if following the strategy would cause price to rise above the MAXIMUM PRICE PREMIUM, then ValueWar constrains the business's ABSOLUTE PRICE so that its price will be no more than MAXIMUM PRICE PREMIUM percentage points above the next-highest competitor. Note: ValueWar looks for the second-highest competitor that's large enough to be noticed, in accordance with the IGNORE SMALL COMPETITORS factor.

The MAXIMUM PRICE DISCOUNT factor follows the same logic but for discount pricing instead of premium pricing. ValueWar will not allow a business to set its prices so low that its price is more than MAXIMUM PRICE DISCOUNT percentage points below the second-lowest competitor.

If a business's competitors do not change their prices, then the business may hit the MAXIMUM PRICE DISCOUNT or PREMIUM limit rather quickly. If one or more of its competitors also changes prices in parallel with the business, then no business may ever be different enough from its competitors to trigger the effects of these factors.

These factors may cause price changes that move a business in the direction opposite to its strategy. However, these factors will not cause a business to abandon its strategic intent. The protective price cuts or increases will stop once the business is within the MAXIMUM PRICE DISCOUNT and PREMIUM bounds. At that point the business will still have the highest or lowest price, as its strategy specified.

A business may stop raising or cutting its price for reasons other than the MAXIMUM PRICE DIFFERENCE factors. Specifically, it might hit limits imposed by the DIFFERENT-ENOUGH PRICE or FEASIBLE CHANGE IN PRICE factors.

Sample value

A value of 10% for MAXIMUM PRICE PREMIUM means that a 10-percentage-point advantage in price is as high as is prudent. In other words, it means that price premiums over 10% (relative to the highest-priced competitor) are uncompetitive.

Legal values   Lower limit: 0%. Upper limit: 400%. These limits apply to both the MAXIMUM PRICE DISCOUNT and MAXIMUM PRICE PREMIUM factors.

Suspending the   If you specify 400%, then ValueWar will essentially ignore these factors.
factor   At 400%, a price premium yields a price five times the nearest competitor's and a discount means a price one-fifth of the nearest competitor's. It is extremely unlikely that a business will reach such levels; thus, setting these factors to 400% will not cause any pricing to be considered uncompetitive.

See also   DIFFERENT-ENOUGH PRICE
                       FEASIBLE CHANGE IN PRICE

Factor: **MAXIMUM QUALITY DIFFERENCE**
MAXIMUM QUALITY INFERIORITY
MAXIMUM QUALITY PREMIUM

Definition

The MAXIMUM QUALITY DIFFERENCE factors determine how much higher or lower a business's quality can be (relative to its competitors') before its quality becomes strategically unacceptable.

What the factor does

A business's RELATIVE QUALITY changes due to its quality actions and its competitors' quality actions. The resulting intended or inadvertent change in RELATIVE QUALITY may make the business's quality unnecessarily high or uncompetitively low.

A real business wouldn't let its quality fall so low that it becomes uncompetitive. ValueWar uses the MAXIMUM QUALITY INFERIORITY factor to prevent a business from failing to satisfy market needs. This factor may override a business's strategy: if following the strategy would cause quality to fall below the MAXIMUM QUALITY INFERIORITY, then ValueWar constrains the business's ABSOLUTE QUALITY so that it will be no more than MAXIMUM QUALITY INFERIORITY points below the next-lowest competitor. Note: ValueWar looks for the second-lowest competitor that's large enough to be noticed, in accordance with the IGNORE SMALL COMPETITORS factor.

The MAXIMUM QUALITY PREMIUM factor follows the same logic but for premium quality instead of "economy" quality. ValueWar will not allow a business to raise its quality so high that its quality is more than MAXIMUM QUALITY PREMIUM points above the second-highest competitor.

If a business's competitors do not change their quality, then the business may hit the MAXIMUM QUALITY INFERIORITY or PREMIUM limit rather quickly. If one or more of its competitors also changes quality in parallel with the business, then no business may ever be different enough from its competitors to trigger the effects of these factors.

These factors may cause quality changes that move a business in the direction opposite to its strategy. However, these factors will not cause a business to abandon its strategic intent. The protective quality cuts or increases will stop once the business is within the MAXIMUM QUALITY INFERIORITY and PREMIUM bounds. At that point the business will still have the highest or lowest quality, as its strategy specified.

A business may stop raising or cutting its quality for reasons other than the MAXIMUM QUALITY DIFFERENCE factors. Specifically, it might hit limits imposed by the DIFFERENT-ENOUGH QUALITY or FEASIBLE CHANGE IN QUALITY factors.

Sample value

A value of 10 for MAXIMUM QUALITY PREMIUM means that a 10-point premium in quality is as high as is necessary. In other words, it means that quality premiums over 10 points are not valued by the market.

Legal values   Lower limit: 0. Upper limit: 100. These limits apply to both the
                       MAXIMUM QUALITY INFERIORITY and PREMIUM factors.

Suspending the   If you specify 100, then ValueWar will generally ignore this factor. It is
factor   extremely unlikely that any competitor will ever reach a position of quality
                       that's 100 points above or below its nearest competitor.

See also   DIFFERENT-ENOUGH QUALITY
                       FEASIBLE CHANGE IN QUALITY

Factor: ORDERED CAPACITY READY IN PERIOD

Definition

ORDERED CAPACITY READY IN PERIOD indicates the period in which CAPACITY ON ORDER will come on stream.

This factor is entered for each competitor.

What the factor does

This factor controls the time at which CAPACITY ON ORDER, if any, becomes available for use.

Sample value

A value of 3 means that the CAPACITY ON ORDER will be ready for use in period 3 (i.e., year 1, quarter 3).

Legal values

Lower limit: 0. Upper limit: 20. Special value: -1 indicates that no capacity is on order. .

Suspending the factor

ValueWar ignores the whole concept of ordered capacity if the ORDERED CAPACITY READY IN PERIOD factor has the value -1. In addition, this factor will have no effect if CAPACITY ON ORDER has the value 0.

See also

CAPACITY ON ORDER

Factor: **PRODUCTIVITY**
PRODUCTIVITY IN FIXED COSTS
PRODUCTIVITY IN VARIABLE COSTS

Definition

PRODUCTIVITY effects can reduce fixed and/or variable costs over time. The PRODUCTIVITY factors specify the rate, if any, at which PRODUCTIVITY improvements make FIXED COSTS and/or VARIABLE COSTS decline.

These factors are entered for each competitor.

What the factor does

The PRODUCTIVITY factors control how fast operating costs decline over time. Thus, they simulate cost-cutting programs, including TQM, that management puts in place.

The two PRODUCTIVITY factors indicate the percentage reduction in FIXED COSTS and VARIABLE COSTS in each period. The two kinds of costs can change at different rates.

Negative numbers mean that PRODUCTIVITY improves over time; that is, they mean that PRODUCTIVITY makes fixed or variable costs go down. Positive numbers mean that costs are expected to rise over time.

ValueWar measures financial data in "real," not inflated, currencies. Thus, the PRODUCTIVITY factors are measured exclusive of inflation.

Sample value

A value of -5% means that PRODUCTIVITY improves (and costs decline) by 5% per period, net of inflation. In more detail: a business that expects a 5% increase in the cost of materials per period (inflation) and also a 5% decrease in the utilization of materials per period (productivity) will have a 5% PRODUCTIVITY improvement, not 0%.

Legal values

Lower limit: -50%. Upper limit: +25%. These limits apply to both factors.

Suspending the factor

ValueWar will simulate no PRODUCTIVITY effects on FIXED COSTS or VARIABLE COSTS if the respective factors are set to 0%.

See also

EXPERIENCE EFFECT
STRUCTURAL CHANGES IN PRICE

Factor: PROFIT

Definition

PROFIT is what's left of SALES (if anything) after subtracting FIXED COSTS and TOTAL VARIABLE COSTS.

This factor is calculated for each business from other factors you enter with the ValueWar Calibrator software.

What the factor does

Along with MARKET SHARE, PROFIT is a key measure of success.

ValueWar measures PROFIT prior to tax and interest expenses. Thus, PROFIT is sensitive only to the effects of strategic changes, not financing decisions.

As in real life, PROFIT in ValueWar results from the interaction of many factors. Competitors with different cost and capacity structures may have radically different PROFIT results even if they follow identical strategies. Changing assumptions about the market itself — for example, about SEASONALITY, growth, or its sensitivity to quality and price — can likewise cause major changes in financial performance even with no change in strategy.

Sample value

A value of 2,000 for PROFIT for a business means that its SALES exceeded its total costs by 2,000 (dollars, lira, yen, or whatever).

Legal values

There are no specific limits on this factor. Legal values on its components ensure that this factor will be meaningful.

Suspending the factor

ValueWar calculates this factor from other factors you enter. You cannot suspend the effect of this factor.

See also

CUMULATIVE PROFITS

Factor: RELATIVE COSTS/UNIT

Definition

RELATIVE COSTS/UNIT measures whether each business is operating at a cost advantage or at a cost disadvantage in each period.

This factor is calculated for each business from the TOTAL COST factor.

What the factor does

RELATIVE COSTS/UNIT shows how much each business spent in total to produce each unit of products and services in a given period, relative to the market average. In other words, it compares each business's TOTAL COSTS to its competitors', on a per-unit-sold basis.

A business with RELATIVE COSTS/UNIT over 100% is operating at a cost disadvantage as compared to its competitors. Under 100% means a cost advantage, and exactly 100% means equivalent costs.

It is important to recognize that different competitors may have radically different cost structures (i.e., different mixes of FIXED and VARIABLE COSTS) and yet look similar with respect to RELATIVE COSTS/UNIT at a point in time.

Sample value

If one business's TOTAL COSTS were 5,000 and UNIT SALES were 100 units, and its three competitors' costs and units were 3,000 for 60, 6,000 for 120, and 4,000 for 80 respectively, then the business had RELATIVE COSTS/UNIT of 100%.

Legal values

There are no specific limits on this factor. Legal values on its components ensure that this factor will be meaningful.

Suspending the factor

ValueWar calculates this factor from other factors you enter. You cannot suspend the effect of this factor.

See also

TOTAL COSTS
UNIT SALES

Factor: RELATIVE PRICE

Definition   RELATIVE PRICE measures each business's price relative to the prices charged by its competitors.

This factor is calculated for each business from the ABSOLUTE PRICE factor you enter with the ValueWar Calibrator software.

What the factor does   A business controls its ABSOLUTE PRICE, but its RELATIVE PRICE depends on its competitors' prices too. Since customers assess RELATIVE PRICE in making purchase decisions, ValueWar puts great emphasis on RELATIVE PRICE in its analyses.

Along with RELATIVE QUALITY, RELATIVE PRICE is a primary driver of MARKET SHARE.

RELATIVE PRICE at the start of ValueWar simulations is determined by initial positions on ABSOLUTE PRICE. Thereafter, RELATIVE PRICE changes as a function of changes in ABSOLUTE PRICE, which in turn are set by the strategies you select for each competitor.

It is very rarely possible to know the "right" RELATIVE PRICE because the "right" price depends on many factors. In fact, since ValueWar allows you to experiment with so many relevant factors, a major reason for using ValueWar is to explore the cost/benefit tradeoffs for different levels of RELATIVE PRICE.

A business with RELATIVE PRICE over 100% is charging a premium relative to its competitors. RELATIVE PRICEs under 100% mean discount pricing. Exactly 100% means matching the average of the market; that is, matching the average of competitors' prices. It is possible to charge a very high ABSOLUTE PRICE and have a low RELATIVE PRICE, and vice versa.

RELATIVE PRICE is calculated for each business in three steps: 1) calculate the average ABSOLUTE PRICE for the four businesses in the market; 2) divide this business's ABSOLUTE PRICE by the average; 3) multiply by 100.0.

Sample value   If one business charges 100 for a product, and its three competitors charge 80, 100, and 120 respectively, then the business has a RELATIVE PRICE of 100%.

Legal values   There are no specific limits on this factor. Legal values on its components ensure that this factor will be meaningful.

Suspending the factor   ValueWar calculates this factor from other factors you enter. You cannot suspend the effect of this factor.

See also   ABSOLUTE PRICE

Factor: RELATIVE QUALITY

Definition

RELATIVE QUALITY measures the quality of each business's products and services relative to the quality offered by its competitors'.

This factor is calculated for each business from the ABSOLUTE QUALITY factor you enter with the ValueWar Calibrator software.

What the factor does

A business controls its ABSOLUTE QUALITY, but its RELATIVE QUALITY depends on its competitors' quality too. Since it is RELATIVE QUALITY that customers assess in making purchase decisions, ValueWar puts great emphasis on RELATIVE QUALITY in its analyses.

Along with RELATIVE PRICE, RELATIVE QUALITY is a primary driver of MARKET SHARE.

RELATIVE QUALITY at the start of ValueWar simulations is determined by initial positions on ABSOLUTE QUALITY. Thereafter, RELATIVE QUALITY changes as a function of changes in ABSOLUTE QUALITY, which in turn are set by the strategies you select for each competitor.

It is very rarely possible to know the "right" RELATIVE QUALITY because what's "right" depends on many factors. In fact, since ValueWar allows you to experiment with so many relevant factors, a major reason for using ValueWar is to explore the cost/benefit tradeoffs for different levels of RELATIVE QUALITY.

ValueWar offers a rich set of tools for simulating the effects of changing RELATIVE QUALITY with different assumptions about the costs or savings of those changes. Thorough discussion of these possibilities are beyond the scope of this book; please feel free to call us with questions. Meanwhile, you might want to explore the EFFECT OF DECREASING QUALITY and the EFFECT OF INCREASING QUALITY factors.

A business with RELATIVE QUALITY over 100% offers premium products and services, relative to its competitors. RELATIVE QUALITY under 100% mean products and services inferior to competitors'. Exactly 100% means matching the average of the market; that is, matching the average of competitors' quality. It is possible to offer a very high ABSOLUTE QUALITY and have a low RELATIVE QUALITY, and vice versa.

RELATIVE QUALITY is calculated for each business in three steps: 1) calculate the average ABSOLUTE QUALITY for the four businesses in the market; 2) divide this business's ABSOLUTE QUALITY by the average; 3) multiply by 100.0.

Sample value

If one business's quality is 50, and its three competitors offer 40, 50, and 60 respectively, then the business has a RELATIVE QUALITY of 100%.

Legal values

There are no specific limits on this factor. Legal values on its components ensure that this factor will be meaningful.

Suspending the factor   ValueWar calculates this factor from other factors you enter. You cannot suspend the effect of this factor.

See also   ABSOLUTE QUALITY
EFFECT OF DECREASING QUALITY ON COSTS
EFFECT OF INCREASING QUALITY ON COSTS

Factor: RESPONSIVENESS TO PRICE

Definition

RESPONSIVENESS TO PRICE expresses the price sensitivity of the market you're simulating with ValueWar.

You can enter up to five values for this factor, which lets you simulate business and economic cycles. See the factor description for MARKET CYCLES for more details.

What the factor does

RESPONSIVENESS TO PRICE controls both the degree to which customers reward sellers for attractive *relative* prices and the degree to which customers care about price versus quality. You can have different values for RESPONSIVENESS TO PRICE for different business cycles, which enables you to say, for example, that customers become more price-sensitive during a recession.

Large values for RESPONSIVENESS TO PRICE indicate that customers care a lot about RELATIVE PRICE. If the value is greater than the RESPONSIVENESS TO QUALITY factor, then customers care more about price than about quality.

Negative numbers for RESPONSIVENESS TO PRICE mean that customers prefer low prices to high prices. Zero means customers don't care at all about price.

ValueWar uses the RESPONSIVENESS TO PRICE and RESPONSIVENESS TO QUALITY factors to control market shares. Businesses will gain market share to the extent that their relative quality or relative price changes in accordance with customers' quality sensitivity and price sensitivity. (ValueWar also uses factors such as CUSTOMER LOYALTY, UNIT CAPACITY, and so on, in estimating market shares.)

Sample value

Compare a value of -1.2, for example, for RESPONSIVENESS TO PRICE to the value for RESPONSIVENESS TO QUALITY to determine whether the market is primarily price sensitive or quality sensitive.

Legal values

Lower limit: -10. Upper limit: 0.

Suspending the factor

If you enter 0, then customers will ignore relative-price differences among competitors as they decide from which to buy.

See also

DEMAND ELASTICITIES
MARKET CYCLES
RESPONSIVENESS TO QUALITY

Factor: RESPONSIVENESS TO QUALITY

Definition

RESPONSIVENESS TO QUALITY expresses the quality sensitivity of the market you're simulating with ValueWar.

You can enter up to five values for this factor, which lets you simulate business and economic cycles. See the factor description for MARKET CYCLES for more details.

What the factor does

RESPONSIVENESS TO QUALITY controls both the degree to which customers reward sellers for attractive quality and the degree to which customers care about quality versus price. You can have different values for RESPONSIVENESS TO QUALITY for different business cycles, which enables you to say, for example, that customers are most quality-sensitive during times of rapid growth.

Large values for RESPONSIVENESS TO QUALITY indicate that customers care a lot about RELATIVE QUALITY. If the value is greater than the RESPONSIVENESS TO PRICE factor, then customers care more about quality than about price.

Positive numbers for RESPONSIVENESS TO QUALITY mean that customers prefer high quality to low quality. Zero means customers don't care at all about quality.

ValueWar uses the RESPONSIVENESS TO QUALITY and RESPONSIVENESS TO PRICE factors to control market shares. Businesses will gain market share to the extent that their RELATIVE QUALITY or RELATIVE PRICE changes in accordance with customers' quality sensitivity and price sensitivity. (ValueWar also uses factors such as CUSTOMER LOYALTY, UNIT CAPACITY, and so on, in estimating market shares.)

Sample value

Compare a value of 1.2, for example, for RESPONSIVENESS TO QUALITY to the value for RESPONSIVENESS TO PRICE to determine whether the market is primarily price sensitive or quality sensitive.

Legal values

Lower limit: 0. Upper limit: 10.

Suspending the factor

If you enter 0, then customers will ignore relative-quality differences among competitors as they decide from which to buy.

See also

DEMAND ELASTICITIES
MARKET CYCLES
RESPONSIVENESS TO PRICE

Factor: RETURN ON SALES (ROS)

Definition

RETURN ON SALES (ROS) is the ratio of PROFIT to SALES.

This factor is calculated for each business from the PROFIT and SALES factors.

What the factor does

ROS is a measure of financial success. Unlike PROFIT, ROS indicates a rate of profitability that's independent of the size of the business.

Note that ROS does not indicate the profitability of the next or previous sale. If SALES were to drop, ROS would probably (but not necessarily) drop because FIXED COSTS would be spread over a smaller sales base. If SALES were to rise, ROS might or might not rise, depending on whether additional CAPACITY were required and depending on the price and quality actions taken to increase SALES.

Sample value

A value of 15% for ROS for a business means that 15% of its SALES went to PROFIT. In other words, it earns 15% PROFIT on every dollar (or mark, krona, etc.) of SALES.

Legal values

There are no specific limits on this factor. Legal values on its components ensure that this factor will be meaningful.

Suspending the factor

ValueWar calculates this factor from other factors you enter. You cannot suspend the effect of this factor.

See also

PROFIT
SALES

Factor: SALES

Definition

SALES is the revenue value of the products or services sold by each business.

This factor is calculated for each business from other factors you enter with the ValueWar Calibrator software. Specifically, it is calculated from ABSOLUTE PRICE, SIZE OF MARKET, and UNIT SHARE.

What the factor does

SALES indicates revenue, as opposed to the number of units sold. It equals ABSOLUTE PRICE times UNIT SALES.

SALES changes over time as a function of many factors. In fact, one of the strengths of ValueWar is that it can simulates changes in SALES quite realistically; in other words, that it simulates future SALES by using sophisticated market models, rather than straight-line extrapolations.

Sample value

A value of 2,000 for SALES for a business means that it recognized revenue of 2,000 (dollars or pounds or francs or whatever).

Legal values

Lower limit: 1. Upper limit: none.

Suspending the factor

ValueWar calculates this factor from other factors you enter. You cannot suspend the effect of this factor.

See also

UNIT SALES

Factor: SCENARIO NAME AND DESCRIPTION

Definition
You can enter text that names and describes the market in your ValueWar simulations. ValueWar displays these names on its screens and reports.

What the factor does
The SCENARIO NAME is the name of the market you're simulating. In the Horse-race scenario in the demo version of ValueWar, the SCENARIO NAME is "Horse race." You can enter a name up to 20 characters long for the scenario.

The SCENARIO DESCRIPTION is text you enter that appears when you press the (F2) key from the scenario menu. You and your colleagues can use this description as a helpful reminder of what you intend to portray with a particular scenario. You may enter up to 14 lines of 80 characters each for the SCENARIO DESCRIPTION.

Sample value
In the Horse-race scenario of the demo version of ValueWar, the SCENARIO NAME is, unsurprisingly, "Horse race."

Legal values
You must supply a SCENARIO NAME for each scenario. The name must be at least 1 and no more than 20 characters long.

You may supply a SCENARIO DESCRIPTION for each scenario. The description, if any, must be no longer than 14 lines of 80 characters each.

Suspending the factor
You must enter a SCENARIO NAME for each scenario. The names you select are used for labeling only; they do not effect ValueWar calculations. You may, but do not have to, enter a SCENARIO DESCRIPTION for any or all of your scenarios.

See also
COMPETITOR NAMES

Factor: SEASONALITY

Definition

SEASONALITY indicates the percentage of SALES that occur in each of the four quarters (periods) of the year. There are four values for the SEASONALITY factor, one for each quarter.

What the factor does

ValueWar uses SEASONALITY to determine how much of the year's SALES occur in each of the year's quarters. You can use this factor to model markets that have seasonal patterns of SALES, such as toys, sun-tan lotion, snow tires, vacation travel, etc.

SEASONALITY works as a modifier to the MARKET GROWTH RATE: it adjusts period-by-period sales to a seasonal trend while still preserving the year-to-year growth (or decline) specified by the growth rate.

Note that SEASONALITY affects market demand but not the businesses' FIXED COSTS. Thus, businesses in highly seasonal markets will find that PROFITS are squeezed in low-demand quarters and CAPACITY might be a constraint in high-demand quarters.

ValueWar considers period 1 to be the first quarter of the year being simulated. If your market has most of its sales in the fourth quarter of the calendar year, and if you start your ValueWar simulations from the summer, then ValueWar's period 1 will be calendar quarter 3. In this case you would enter a high number for SEASONALITY in quarter 2, not quarter 4.

Sample value

Values of 10%, 20%, 20%, and 50% for quarters 1 through 4 would indicate a very seasonal market, one in which half of the SALES occur in the last quarter of the year.

Legal values

Lower limit: 0%. Upper limit: 100%. When added together, the four SEASONALITY factors must total 100%.

Suspending the factor

You can specify a non-seasonal market by entering 25% for each of the four quarters' SEASONALITY.

See also

CAPACITY TRIGGER POINT
DEMAND ELASTICITIES
SIZE OF MARKET

Factor: SIZE OF MARKET

Definition

SIZE OF MARKET expresses the total market demand, in units, for the period at the start of the ValueWar simulation.

What the factor does

SIZE OF MARKET sets the beginning point for ValueWar simulations. The MARKET GROWTH RATE and DEMAND ELASTICITIES factors control how the market size changes over time.

SIZE OF MARKET is measured for one period; that is, for one quarter of the year. It is measured for the period that ValueWar calls period 0.

ValueWar uses SIZE OF MARKET as the fundamental demand from which to infer demand in subsequent periods. If actual data for period 0 is unusual in the sense that it has been distorted by unusually low or high demand, you might want to adjust the SIZE OF MARKET to a more-representative number.

Sample value

A value of 125,000 means that customers in the market purchased a total of 125 thousand units of products or services in the period at the start of the ValueWar simulation.

Legal values

Lower limit: 1. Upper limit: none.

Suspending the factor

You cannot suspend the effect of this factor.

See also

DEMAND ELASTICITIES
MARKET GROWTH RATE

Factor: STRUCTURAL CHANGE IN PRICE

Definition

STRUCTURAL CHANGE IN PRICE refers to market or industry trends in ABSOLUTE PRICE that all competitors follow, regardless of their strategies. It simulates general evolution in prices.

What the factor does

STRUCTURAL CHANGE IN PRICE lets ValueWar capture general trends that all competitors in a market "obey." For example, in the computer and consumer electronics industries, virtually all manufacturers reduce prices over time, which is what ValueWar considers a structural change.

Competitors' strategies result in changes to price above or below the trend established by the structural change. Thus, competitors' changes in ABSOLUTE PRICE are the net effect of the structural change and the effects caused by their strategies.

STRUCTURAL CHANGE IN PRICE is measured exclusive of inflation. In other words, ValueWar assumes that all financial measures are in "real" values, not inflated values, and that the structural change captures price changes above or below the general rate of inflation. Thus, if market prices tend to rise in concert with inflation, then it is proper to use a value of 0 for this factor.

A negative number for STRUCTURAL CHANGE IN PRICE means that price falls instead of rises from period to period.

ValueWar will not let ABSOLUTE PRICE exceed the bounds defined by the FEASIBLE PRICE factors no matter what the value of the STRUCTURAL CHANGE IN PRICE factor.

Sample value

A value of -5 means that all competitors' ABSOLUTE PRICE will fall by 5 percent per period before taking their strategies into account. Their strategies will result in changes above or below the 5-percent structural change. As discussed above, -5 means 5 percentage points below the rate of inflation.

Legal values

Lower limit: -50%. Upper limit: +50%.

Suspending the factor

A value of 0 makes ValueWar disregard this factor. With a value of 0, the only changes in competitors' price will result from their choices of strategy and from the MAXIMUM PRICE DISCOUNT and PREMIUM factors.

See also

MAXIMUM PRICE DISCOUNT
MAXIMUM PRICE PREMIUM
STRUCTURAL CHANGE IN QUALITY

Factor: STRUCTURAL CHANGE IN QUALITY

Definition

STRUCTURAL CHANGE IN QUALITY refers to market or industry trends in ABSOLUTE QUALITY that all competitors follow, regardless of their strategies. It simulates general evolution in products or services.

What the factor does

STRUCTURAL CHANGE IN QUALITY lets ValueWar capture general trends that all competitors in a market "obey." For example, in the computer and consumer electronics industries, virtually all manufacturers score steady improvements in ABSOLUTE QUALITY, which is what ValueWar considers a structural change.

Competitors' strategies result in changes to quality above or below the trend established by the structural change. Thus, competitors' changes in ABSOLUTE QUALITY are the net effect of the structural change and the effects caused by their strategies.

A negative number for STRUCTURAL CHANGE IN QUALITY means that quality falls instead of rises from period to period.

ValueWar will not let ABSOLUTE QUALITY exceed the bounds defined by the FEASIBLE QUALITY factors no matter what the value of the STRUCTURAL CHANGE IN QUALITY factor.

Sample value

A value of 5 means that all competitors' ABSOLUTE QUALITY will rise by 5 points per period before taking their strategies into account. Their strategies will result in changes above or below the 5-point structural change.

Legal values

Lower limit: -20. Upper limit: +20.

Suspending the factor

A value of 0 makes ValueWar disregard this factor. With a value of 0, the only changes in competitors' quality will result from their choices of strategy and from the MAXIMUM QUALITY INFERIORITY and PREMIUM factors.

See also

MAXIMUM QUALITY INFERIORITY
MAXIMUM QUALITY PREMIUM
STRUCTURAL CHANGE IN PRICE

Factor:	**SUPPLY/DEMAND TRIGGERS**
	CUT-PRICE TRIGGER
	STOP-CUTTING TRIGGER
	RAISE-PRICE TRIGGER
	STOP-RAISING TRIGGER

Definition

The SUPPLY/DEMAND TRIGGERS control the P BY SUPPLY/ DEMAND strategy. As described in the *Strategy Reference*, this strategy tries to manage supply and demand for a business by balancing prices and capacity utilization. The four trigger points determine how that balance occurs.

These factors have no effect on businesses that don't adopt the P BY SUPPLY/DEMAND strategy. The rest of this description of the factors applies only to businesses following that strategy.

What the factor does

The CUT-PRICE TRIGGER controls when ValueWar cuts prices. If CAPACITY UTILIZATION falls below this trigger, then ValueWar will cut prices in order to increase demand (and capacity utilization).

The STOP-CUTTING TRIGGER controls when ValueWar will stop the price-cutting described above. Imagine a business that has cut price because its CAPACITY UTILIZATION fell below the CUT-PRICE TRIGGER, and imagine that the price cut worked and utilization went back up. When utilization rises above the CUT-PRICE TRIGGER and stays below the STOP-CUTTING TRIGGER, prices will hold steady; they will stop being cut. Prices will rise toward their pre-cut levels if utilization rises above the STOP-CUTTING TRIGGER.

The RAISE-PRICE TRIGGER controls when ValueWar raises prices. If CAPACITY UTILIZATION rises above this trigger, then ValueWar will raise prices in order to not "leave money on the table" during times of peak demand.

The STOP-RAISING TRIGGER is exactly analogous to the STOP-CUTTING TRIGGER. It controls when price increases stop (which is when utilization gets between the STOP-RAISING and the RAISE-PRICE TRIGGERs) and when prices go back to normal (which is when utilization gets between the STOP-CUTTING and STOP-RAISING TRIGGERs).

ValueWar will not let ABSOLUTE PRICE exceed the bounds defined by the FEASIBLE PRICE factors no matter what actions happen due to the SUPPLY/DEMAND TRIGGER POINT factors.

Sample value

A value of 0.70 for the CUT-PRICE TRIGGER means that ValueWar will cause a competitor to cut its ABSOLUTE PRICE if its CAPACITY UTILIZATION falls below 70% (assuming that the competitor is following the P BY SUPPLY/DEMAND strategy).

Legal values

Lower limit: 0.01. Upper limit: 1.00. These limits apply to all of the SUPPLY/DEMAND TRIGGER POINT factors. In addition, the triggers must be in a logical order; the STOP-CUTTING TRIGGER, for example, must not be below the CUT-PRICE TRIGGER.

Suspending the factor   Use extreme values to prevent one or more of these factors from having any influence over the P BY SUPPLY/DEMAND strategy. These factors will have no influence at all for businesses that don't follow that strategy.

See also   CAPACITY UTILIZATION
CAPACITY TRIGGER POINT
DEBOTTLENECKING CAPACITY
FEASIBLE PRICE

Factor:	**TIME BETWEEN MOVES**
	TIME BETWEEN PRICE MOVES
	TIME BETWEEN QUALITY MOVES

Definition

The TIME BETWEEN MOVES factors let ValueWar simulate situations in which businesses cannot change quality or price in every period.

Both factors are entered for each competitor.

What the factor does

These factors control how many periods must elapse between quality or price actions. ValueWar uses these factors to simulate the effects of planning cycles, management attention, desires to avoid frequent product or price changes, and so on.

TIME BETWEEN MOVES is measured in periods. Thus, a value of 3 for TIME BETWEEN QUALITY MOVES means that a business must wait 3 periods after it raises or lowers its quality before it can make another change. A value of 0 means that a business that altered its price in period 5 may also alter it in period 6 (a delay of 0 periods).

You can force quality and price to change simultaneously. If you specify -1 for a business's TIME BETWEEN PRICE MOVES factor, then that business cannot change price on a different schedule from when it changes quality. For example, if such a business changed its quality in period 5 and if it had a 3-period quality-moves delay, then it could change neither its quality nor its price until period 9.

ValueWar makes the following exceptions to these time delays: 1) non-strategy moves override these factors, thereby allowing quality and/or price changes before the delays have elapsed; 2) quality or price moves may occur that are forced by the MAXIMUM PRICE DIFFERENCE and MAXIMUM QUALITY DIFFERENCE factors, even if those moves violate these time delays.

Sample value

A value of 0 means the fastest possible action. In other words, 0 means that a business can act in every period.

Legal values

Lower limit: 0. Upper limit: 20. These limits apply to both factors, except that TIME BETWEEN PRICE MOVES also accepts the special value of -1 to synchronize quality and price moves.

Suspending the factor

If you specify 0 for all competitors, then ValueWar will essentially ignore this factor. All competitors will make quality and price moves as often as they wish.

See also

CUSTOMER PERCEPTION TIME
FIRST POSSIBLE MOVE
TIME TO MAKE/PERCEIVE MOVES

Factor: **TIME TO MAKE/PERCEIVE MOVES**
TIME TO MAKE/PERCEIVE PRICE MOVES
TIME TO MAKE/PERCEIVE QUALITY MOVES

Definition   TIME TO MAKE/PERCEIVE MOVES lets ValueWar simulate the time it takes for businesses to change quality and price and the time it takes for businesses to perceive that their competitors have changed their quality and price.

Both factors are entered for each competitor.

What the factor does   These factors control the time lag between the period in which a business decides to make a quality or price change and the period in which that change actually happens. ValueWar uses these factors to simulate R&D cycles, delays in market research or competitive intelligence, and so on.

TIME TO MAKE/PERCEIVE MOVES is measured in periods. Thus, a value of 3 means that it would take a business 3 periods to change its quality or price once it decided to make that change. For example, if that business was following a HIGHEST Q & P strategy (see the Strategy *Reference* section), and if it determined that a competitor had beaten its quality, then it would take 3 periods for the business to respond with a quality improvement of its own. Alternatively (and equivalently), a value of 3 would also simulate that the business does not know for 3 periods that its quality has been beaten, but then it responds immediately.

These factors also affect strategies that look at competitors' results, such as FOLLOW SUCCESS. They determine how far in the past a business using such a strategy will look to assess its competitors' performance.

These factors are particularly interesting in markets where different competitors require different amounts of TIME TO MAKE/PERCEIVE MOVES. You could observe the effect of speedy response times by, for example, calibrating one scenario with equal response times for all competitors, and another in which one or more competitors move faster than others.

You can use these factors to test easy-to-copy quality moves versus hard-to-copy moves. In the easy-to-copy scenario, you'd have rapid response times (values at or near 0) for competitors; in the hard-to-copy scenario, you'd have slower response times.

Sample value   A value of 0 means immediate action and perception. In other words, 0 means that a business can react in the period immediately following one in which one or more of its competitors makes a quality or price change.

Legal values   Lower limit: 0. Upper limit: 20. These limits apply to both factors.

Suspending the factor   If you specify 0 for all competitors, then ValueWar will essentially ignore these factors. All competitors will perceive and react to quality and price changes as quickly as possible.

See also   CUSTOMER PERCEPTION TIME
FIRST POSSIBLE MOVE
TIME BETWEEN MOVES

Factor: TOTAL COSTS

Definition

TOTAL COSTS is the sum of FIXED COSTS and TOTAL VARIABLE COSTS. It expresses the total cost of operating each business.

This factor is calculated for each business from other factors.

What the factor does

TOTAL COSTS is used to calculate PROFIT and to compare the cost structures of the businesses in the ValueWar simulation.

Different businesses may have identical TOTAL COSTS but have very different cost structures. One might have predominantly FIXED COSTS, another might have mostly VARIABLE COSTS, and another might have some of each. Thus, your cost analysis should usually look at those details rather than at TOTAL COSTS alone.

Since TOTAL COSTS will depend largely on the size of the business, there are no "good" or "bad" values for it.

Sample value

A value of 50,000 for TOTAL COSTS in one period for a business means that it spent 50,000 to operate and to produce products and services in that period.

Legal values

There are no specific limits on this factor. Legal values on its components ensure that this factor will be meaningful.

Suspending the factor

ValueWar calculates this factor from other factors you enter. You cannot suspend the effect of this factor.

See also

RELATIVE COSTS/UNIT

Factor: TOTAL VARIABLE COSTS

Definition

TOTAL VARIABLE COSTS equals total expenses in each period that are dependent on unit-sales volume.

This factor is calculated for each business from other factors. Specifically, it equals UNIT SALES times VARIABLE COSTS PER UNIT.

What the factor does

TOTAL VARIABLE COSTS represent part of each business's cost structure. The other part is FIXED COSTS. ValueWar uses TOTAL VARIABLE COSTS along with SALES and FIXED COSTS to calculate PROFIT.

Sample value

A business with a value of 5,000 for UNIT SALES and VARIABLE COSTS PER UNIT of 1.50 will have TOTAL VARIABLE COSTS of 7,500.

Legal values

There are no specific limits on this factor. Legal values on its components ensure that this factor will be meaningful.

Suspending the factor

ValueWar calculates this factor from other factors you enter. You cannot suspend the effect of this factor.

See also

VARIABLE COSTS PER UNIT

Factor: UNIT DEMAND

Definition

UNIT DEMAND is the number of units of products or services that customers in the market would like to buy from each business.

This factor is calculated for each business from other factors.

What the factor does

UNIT DEMAND indicates potential sales in "real" (i.e., without the effects of price) terms. It depends on CUSTOMER LOYALTY, CUSTOMER TRIALS, MARKET GROWTH RATE, UNIT SHARE in previous periods, and so on.

UNIT SALES will be lower than UNIT DEMAND for businesses that have insufficient CAPACITY to satisfy demand for their products or services.

A business's UNIT SALES may be higher than UNIT DEMAND if one or more of its competitors has insufficient CAPACITY to meet its demand. In such cases, ValueWar distributes the unmet demand to the other competitors as though the unmet demand was a miniature market in which the capacity-constrained competitor does not participate. In other words, ValueWar actually assesses RELATIVE PRICE, RELATIVE QUALITY, MARKET SHARE, and so on, for the competitors who have enough CAPACITY, and it uses the results to decide how much of the unmet demand goes to each of those competitors. ValueWar repeats this process until all the unmet demand is satisfied or until all competitors run out of CAPACITY.

Sample value

A value of 2,000 for UNIT DEMAND for a business means that its customers wanted to buy 2,000 units of products or services.

Legal values

There are no specific limits on this factor. Legal values on its components ensure that this factor will be meaningful.

Suspending the factor

ValueWar calculates this factor from other factors you enter. You cannot suspend the effect of this factor.

See also

UNIT SALES

Factor: UNIT SALES

Definition

UNIT SALES is the number of units of products or services sold by each business.

This factor is calculated for each business from other factors you enter with the ValueWar Calibrator software. Specifically, it is calculated from SIZE OF MARKET and UNIT SHARE.

What the factor does

UNIT SALES indicates sales in "real" (i.e., without the effects of price) terms. It equals the lower of UNIT DEMAND and CAPACITY in any given period. UNIT DEMAND, in turn, is a function of CUSTOMER LOYALTY, CUSTOMER DISLOYALTY, MARKET GROWTH RATE, UNIT SHARE in previous periods, and so on.

UNIT SALES will be lower than UNIT DEMAND for businesses that have insufficient CAPACITY to satisfy demand for their products or services.

A business's UNIT SALES may be higher than UNIT DEMAND if one or more of its competitors has insufficient CAPACITY to meet its demand. In such cases, ValueWar distributes the unmet demand to the other competitors as though the unmet demand was a miniature market in which the capacity-constrained competitor does not participate. In other words, ValueWar actually assesses RELATIVE PRICE, RELATIVE QUALITY, MARKET SHARE, and so on, for the competitors who have enough CAPACITY, and it uses the results to decide how much of the unmet demand goes to each of those competitors. ValueWar repeats this process until all the unmet demand is satisfied or until all competitors run out of CAPACITY.

Sample value

A value of 2,000 for UNIT SALES for a business means that it sold 2,000 units of products or services at the start of the simulation.

Legal values

There are no specific limits on this factor. Legal values on its components ensure that this factor will be meaningful.

Suspending the factor

ValueWar calculates this factor from other factors you enter. You cannot suspend the effect of this factor.

See also

SALES
UNIT DEMAND

Factor: UNIT SHARE

Definition

UNIT SHARE is the percentage of customer purchases captured by each competitor. It is just like market share except that it is measured in terms of units, not revenue.

This factor is entered for each competitor.

What the factor does

UNIT SHARE indicates the initial position of each business's relative size, with "size" measured by UNIT SALES. From it and other factors ValueWar calculates data for other factors.

UNIT SHARE changes over time as businesses gain or lose UNIT SALES as determined by changes to their RELATIVE QUALITY and RELATIVE PRICE and as constrained by various factors such as ELIGIBILITY, FEASIBLE CHANGES IN QUALITY, and so on.

Sample value

A value of 12% for UNIT SHARE for a business means that it had 12% of the market's unit sales at the start of the simulation.

Legal values

Lower limit: 1%. Upper limit: 100%.

Suspending the factor

You cannot suspend the effect of this factor.

See also

MARKET SHARE

Factor: VARIABLE COSTS PER UNIT

Definition   VARIABLE COSTS PER UNIT are all costs incurred as a normal part of doing business and that vary with UNIT SALES or production volume.

This factor is entered for each competitor.

What the factor does   VARIABLE COSTS PER UNIT describes part of each business's cost structure for ValueWar. It includes such volume-dependent expenses as the cost of goods sold, sales commissions, and so on.

Along with the FIXED COSTS factor, VARIABLE COSTS PER UNIT sets the initial value for each business's cost structure at the start of the ValueWar simulations. VARIABLE COSTS PER UNIT can change over time as a result of the EXPERIENCE EFFECT and PRODUCTIVITY, and as a result of changes in QUALITY.

ValueWar will not let ABSOLUTE PRICE fall below VARIABLE COSTS.

The nature of a business's cost structure — that is, its mix of fixed and variable costs, and the amount of each — is crucial not only to its financial performance but also to understanding its strategic motives. For example, a business with relatively high FIXED COSTS will be very sensitive to sales volume and SEASONALITY, whereas a business with relatively high VARIABLE COSTS PER UNIT will be more sensitive to prices. You can use ValueWar to see how changes in quality and price can affect your competitors in ways substantially different from their effects on your business.

Sample value   A value of 100 for a business means that its VARIABLE COSTS PER UNIT start at 100 per unit when the simulation begins.

Legal values   Lower limit: 0. Upper limit: none.

Suspending the factor   You cannot suspend the effect of this factor.

See also   EFFECT OF DECREASING QUALITY ON COSTS
EFFECT OF INCREASING QUALITY ON COSTS
EXPERIENCE EFFECT
FIXED COSTS
PRODUCTIVITY
TOTAL VARIABLE COSTS

Strategy Reference

ValueWar's market strategies express a wide range of strategic intent and motivations. By selecting appropriate strategies for the businesses in the market you're simulating, you can explore an array of business behavior unmatched by other strategy-analysis techniques. Even without using non-strategy moves and without switching strategies for any business during the simulation, you can test tens of thousands of combinations of strategies for each scenario!

ValueWar's operations strategies are described via the multitude of factors that describe scenarios. For example, operations strategies cover cost structures, time required to respond to competitors' actions, costs and savings associated with changing quality, and so on. Market strategies (which control quality and price) and operations strategies together determine each business's competitive strategy.

This section of *Strategy Analysis with ValueWar* provides detailed descriptions of the market strategies from which you can choose.[1] The first part of this section covers the "standard" market strategies; the second part covers "optional" strategies and how to use them. The factor descriptions earlier in the *Reference* section cover operations strategies (as well as the market/customer environment).

We can divide market strategies into three basic types: egocentric, aggressive, and reactive.

Characteristics of all Value-War strategies

> Note: all of ValueWar's strategies obey three basic rules laid down by the values you specify with scenario factors. One: they all ensure that each business's absolute quality or absolute price stays within the limits set by the "feasible quality" and "feasible price" factors. Two: they all ensure that each business's quality and price stays reasonably competitive by holding within the "maximum quality differences" and "maximum price differences" factors. Three: they don't count any "structural changes" in quality or price. Though the *Strategy Reference* section will not repeat these three rules, please remember that they apply to all the strategies listed below.
>
> The result of enforcing these rules may be for businesses to apparently disobey the dictates of their strategies. They're not; they're simply obeying a higher authority.

---

[1] If you find you need to simulate a strategy that ValueWar does not offer, please contact us and we'll see if we can add it to ValueWar for you.

> For more detail on scenario factors, please refer to the *Scenario Reference* section of this book.

Egocentric strategies

Egocentric strategies are the simplest because they do not take into account the actions or reactions of the other competitors in the market. These strategies in effect think of themselves as engaging in an exclusive relationship with the customer, one in which their competitors do not even exist. Consequently, businesses following these strategies set forth toward their targets and don't worry about whether their competitors are matching their moves, moving in the opposite direction, or anything in between.

These strategies are not bound by the "time to perceive moves" factor since they don't have to check competitors' positions.

Despite their blindness, egocentric strategies do not necessarily perform badly (or well). They can have major advantages: they act quickly and they don't get complacent or think they're doing "well enough." Whether these traits turn out to be assets or liabilities depends on the market and on their competitors.

Raise Q and P

A business following this strategy will raise its absolute quality and its absolute price in every period, no matter what actions its competitors take. It will continue to raise quality and price until the end of the simulation is reached (or until the "three basic rules" override the strategy; see the note above).

Raise Q, lag P

This strategy is a variation on Raise Q and P. This one offers greater value to the customer because prices are raised one period later than quality. In other words, quality increases precede price increases by one period.

Don't change Q or P

The simplest strategy of all: don't change absolute quality or absolute price, no matter what happens. (Of course, *relative* quality and *relative* price will change if competitors change *their* quality and price.) Remember, though, that this strategy, like all others, may be overridden by the "three basic rules" described above.

P by supply/demand

This strategy tries to balance pricing and capacity utilization. If capacity utilization gets too low — that is, if supply exceeds demand by a lot — then a business following this strategy will cut its price in an attempt to get the factory running. If capacity utilization gets too high — in other words, if there's barely enough supply (or not enough supply) to meet demand — than a business following this strategy will raise its price in an attempt to not leave money on the table. The points at which the price cuts and price increases (as well as the points at which prices return to "normal") are controlled by various supply/demand "trigger" points.

A business following this strategy does not change its quality unless forced to do so by the "three basic rules" described above.

Aggressive strategies

These market strategies are called "aggressive" because they make the first move, not because they are necessarily belligerent. Businesses that adopt aggressive strategies don't wait to see what their competitors have done; they act first.

The main difference between egocentric strategies and aggressive strategies is that the latter *may* stop changing quality or price while the former will continue changing ad infinitum. But the aggressive strategies won't necessarily stop. For example, if the aggressive Highest Q and P strategy plays against the egocentric Raise Q and P strategy, Highest Q and P will probably act just like Raise Q and P. The reason: depending on their constraints and initial positions, the Highest Q and P strategy may never be able to get higher than the Raise Q and P strategy, even if it increases quality and price in every period.

> The interaction of the Highest Q and P and the Raise Q and P strategies shows how one strategy's *behavior* may be indistinguishable from anothers' under certain circumstances even though its *motives* may be quite different. However, it is vital in strategy analysis to understand the motives as much as the behavior. You might adopt a different strategy for your business if you have reason to believe that a competitor will stop making changes at some point than if you believe that competitor will continue to go higher and higher (or lower and lower).

Unlike the egocentric strategies, the aggressive strategies take their competitors' actions and reactions into account. These strategies want to become "highest" or "lowest" at something, and to do so they must compare their positions against their competitors'. These strategies are affected a great deal by the "different-enough quality," "different-enough price," and "time to perceive moves" scenario factors.

These strategies seem to imply leadership roles that may or may not be a good thing. A business following an aggressive strategy can indeed lead its competitors (depending on their strategies, of course), and it will not have the disadvantage of waiting for others to act first. On the other hand, aggressive strategies make it easier for markets to degenerate into price wars, for example.

All the aggressive strategies follow the "two basic rules" described above. In addition, all aggressive strategies look only at those competitors who are large enough to be "noticed," as controlled by the "ignore small competitors" scenario factor. Competitors with market shares below that threshold are not considered when a business with an aggressive strategy determines whether it has attained the highest (or lowest) quality or price in its market. If no competitor is large enough to be noticed, then aggressive strategies do not change quality or price.

When the aggressive strategies examine their competitive positions, their observations of their competitors are affected by the "time to perceive moves" scenario factor. This factor may cause these strategies to gauge their progress against outdated perceptions of their competitors. Thus, a competitor may think it has achieved the highest-quality position, whereas it may in fact have been overtaken by a competitor whose information is more recent.

Highest Q and P

A business following this strategy will raise both absolute quality and absolute price until they're the highest in the market. If either quality or price is already the highest, then the business will raise just the other one.

This strategy stops raising quality and price when they are "high enough," as determined by the "different-enough quality" and "different-enough price" scenario factors.

Highest Q, steady P

This strategy behaves just like Highest Q and P except that it operates only on quality; it leaves absolute price unchanged.

Highest Q, average P

A business following this strategy will raise its absolute quality until it's the highest in the market (if it ever gets that high). If its quality is already the highest, it will not raise it any further. Increases in quality stop when the quality advantage is "enough".

Meanwhile, a business following this strategy will try to set its price equal to the market average. Thus, it seeks to offer superior quality at a competitive price.

Lowest Q and P

This strategy behaves exactly like Highest Q and P except that the direction is reversed: it cuts quality and price, and it stops cutting when quality and price are the lowest in the market. If either quality or price is already the lowest, then this strategy cuts only the other one. "Lowest" is determined by the "different-enough quality" and "different-enough price" scenario factors.

Steady Q, lowest P

A business following this strategy will cut its absolute price until it's the lowest in the market; it leaves absolute quality unchanged. If its price is already the lowest, then it doesn't cut price any further. "Lowest" is determined by the "different-enough quality" and "different-enough price" scenario factors.

Lead Q and P up

This strategy is primarily aggressive but it has a reactive side to it. It has the business raise both quality and price immediately. After it makes its move, it waits and observes what its competitors did. If any competitor raised quality, this business raises quality again; if no competitor raised quality but at least one held quality constant, this business holds its quality steady (at the raised level); if all its competitors cut quality, then this business cuts quality too. The business makes changes in price by following the same logic.

In other words, a business following this strategy tries to lead quality and price up. If others follow, the business keeps raising quality and/or price; if none respond, then this business holds still and hopes that the others will eventually follow it; if the others go down, the business gives up and follows them down.

Reactive strategies

Reactive strategies never make the first move. Businesses with reactive strategies look at what their competitors are doing (or accomplishing) before they decide how to act.

Reactive strategies have little inherent preference for high or low quality or for high or low price. They're motivated more by doing what seems to work well ... or by doing what seems safe.

In fact, reactive strategies may *never* make a change to quality or price. If all the businesses in a market follow Tit for Best Tat, for example, none will make a first move, and so none will have anything to which to react! As discussed above, it's important for businesses competing in such markets to recognize what really motivates their competitors. Are they following Don't Change Q or P or are they following Tit for Best Tat?

The danger in aggressive strategies is that they can lead to all-out warfare; the danger in reactive strategies is that their hesitation to act can lead to lackluster performance.

Reactive strategies can be highly cooperative. Rather than making provocative first moves, they can observe what seems to work in their market and go along with that behavior. Thus, they have a good chance of avoiding destructive price wars … unless an egocentric or aggressive strategy starts the ball rolling in the wrong direction.

Reactive strategies generally minimize risk because they wait and see what their competitors do. Even so, they can perform almost as well as the competitors they emulate. But it is possible for a reactive strategy to perform very poorly. If two competitors adopt diametrically opposing strategies, and if they run neck and neck for the highest market share, then a business using the Match #1's Q and P strategy may vacillate between the two and get stuck in a poor middle position.

All the reactive strategies follow the "two basic rules" described above. In addition, all reactive strategies look only at those competitors who are large enough to be "noticed," as controlled by the "ignore small competitors" scenario factor. Competitors with market shares below that threshold are not considered when a business with a reactive strategy determines whom to follow. If no competitor is large enough to be noticed, then reactive strategies do not change quality or price.

When the reactive strategies examine their competitive positions, their observations of their competitors are affected by the "time to perceive moves" scenario factor. This factor may cause these strategies to gauge their progress against outdated perceptions of their competitors. Thus, a competitor may think it has matched the position of the most-successful competitor, whereas that competitor may no longer be the most successful.

Match #1's Q and P

A business with this strategy tries to match the absolute quality and absolute price of the competitor who has the largest market share. If the business with this strategy itself has the largest share, it doesn't change its quality or price.

Beat #1's price

This strategy is reactive but it has aggressive overtones. A business following this strategy will try to match the absolute quality while undercutting the absolute price of the competitor with the largest market share. If the business with this strategy already has the largest share, it doesn't change its quality or price.

This strategy deems its price sufficiently lower than the business with the largest share when its discount position satisfies the "different-enough price" scenario factor.

Follow success

A business following this strategy will try to match the absolute quality and absolute price attained by the competitor with the highest profits. If the business itself has the highest profits, it will maintain its quality and price.

Match market average

This strategy makes its adherent try to attain a quality and price position that equals the average quality and average price of the other businesses in the market. The quality and price of the business with this strategy are not included in the market average.

Tit for best tat

A business following Tit for Best Tat takes no action on absolute quality or absolute price unless one or more competitors change quality or price. If any competitor does act, then the business tries to match the quality and price of the most profitable among those who made changes.

A simpler version of this strategy, called Tit for Tat, has been the subject of considerable study in two-player competitions based on the Prisoner's Dilemma. That research (*The Evolution of Cooperation*, by Robert Axelrod) demonstrated that reactive/cooperative strategies can perform well against a wide variety of opponents. The research also helped inspire the creation of ValueWar.

Optional strategies

The strategies described above are ValueWar's "standard" market strategies. Those strategies are the ones normally available to you via the strategy menu when you run ValueWar.

ValueWar also makes available a series of "optional" market strategies. You can replace one or more standard strategies with one or more optional strategies using the procedure described at the end of this section. The optional strategies combine some aspects of egocentric, aggressive, and reactive moves. As with the standard strategies, all the optional strategies obey the "three basic rules" described earlier.

Raise Q, cut P

This strategy is a variation on Raise Q and P. Instead of raising price, however, this strategy cuts price. A business following this strategy will raise its absolute quality and cut its absolute price in every period, no matter what actions its competitors take. Such a business is trying to improve its value at the fastest possible rate.

Steady Q, raise P

A business following this strategy will raise its absolute price every period, no matter what its competitors do; it leaves absolute quality unchanged.

Highest Q, raise P

A business following this strategy will raise its absolute quality until it's the highest in the market (if it ever gets that high). If its quality is already the highest, it will not raise it any further. Increases in quality stop when the quality advantage is "enough".

Meanwhile, a business following this strategy will raise its price every period, no matter what its competitors do. So, this strategy pushes quality up until it's the best, but it pushes prices up forever.

Highest Q, #1's P

This strategy behaves like Highest Q, average P except that it seeks to match the price of the competitor with the largest market share, rather than trying to match the average price in the market.

Highest Q, lag P

This strategy is similar to Raise Q, lag P. The difference is that Raise Q, lag P will cause a business to raise its quality as long as it's able, without regard to competitors' responses, while Highest Q, lag P will stop raising its quality when (and if) its quality is the highest in the market. How high is high enough is determined by the "different-enough quality" factor.

Steady Q, average P

This strategy is like Steady Q, lowest P except for its price objective. Steady Q, lowest P holds quality steady and tries to get the low-price position; Steady Q, average P instead tries to set its price at the market average.

Using optional strategies

You can have ValueWar use optional strategies instead of standard strategies by using the /STRATEGY switch when you start ValueWar. You do not have to use the /STRATEGY switch if the standard strategies are appropriate for your analysis.

All ValueWar strategies have numbers, as shown in the table below. You use those numbers with the /STRATEGY switch to tell ValueWar which strategies you want to use and in what order you want them to appear. You may select between 2 and 15 strategies each time you run ValueWar.

Here are some examples of using the /STRATEGY switch:

VW /STRATEGY=1,2,3,4,5,6,7,8,9,10
(Use standard strategies 1 through 10. Notice that you end up with just 10 strategies.)

VW /STRATEGY=5,4,3,2,1,20,21
(Use standard strategies 1 through 5, in "reverse" order from the usual, plus optional strategies 20 and 21.)

VW /STRATEGY=16,17,18,19,20,21
(Use only the 6 optional strategies.)

Please note that you must spell out the word "strategy" completely, and you must not put any spaces between the switch and any of the strategy numbers.

If you have favorite sets of strategies, you may want to set up DOS "BAT" (batch) files to save yourself the trouble of typing the /STRATEGY switch whenever you want to use one of those sets. Please refer to your DOS documentation for more information about BAT files.

Strategy number	Strategy	Strategy number	Strategy
1	Don't change Q or P	12	Beat #1's price
2	Highest Q and P	13	Lead Q and P up
3	Highest Q, steady P	14	Follow success
4	Steady Q, lowest P	15	Tit for best tat
5	Raise Q and P	16	Raise Q, cut P
6	Raise Q, lag P	17	Steady Q, raise P
7	Lowest Q and P	18	Highest Q, raise P
8	P by supply/demand	19	Highest Q, #1's P
9	Highest Q, average P	20	Highest Q, lag P
10	Match mkt average	21	Steady Q, average P
11	Match #1's Q and P		

Keyboard Reference

Key	Keyboard reference by view							
	Quality/ price	Graph	Data history	Finan. snapsht	Profit and loss	Compe- tition	Scenario test	Strategy test
F1	Help system	Help system	Help system	Help system	Help system	Help system	Help system	Help system
F2	Define data	Define data	Define data	Define data	Define data	Define data	Define data	Define data
F3	New scenario	New scenario	New scenario	New scenario	New scenario	New scenario	*	*
F4	New strategies	New strategies	New strategies	New strategies	New strategies	New strategies	*	*
F5	Test scenario	Test scenario	Test scenario	Test scenario	Test scenario	Test scenario	NA	*
F6	Test strategies	Test strategies	Test strategies	Test strategies	Test strategies	Test strategies	*	Test strategies
F7	Non-strat move	Non-strat move	Non-strat move	Non-strat move	Non-strat move	Non-strat move	*	*
F8	(Unused)	(Unused)	(Unused)	(Unused)	(Unused)	(Unused)	(Unused)	(Unused)
F9	Report	Report	Report	Report	Report	Report	Report	Report
F10 TAB SHIFT - TAB	Animate	Animate						
↑↓	Change period	Change period	Change period	Change data	Change data	Change data	Change period	Change period
←→	Change data	Change data	Change data	Change period	Change period	Change period	Change data	Change data
HOME END	First, last period	First, last period	First, last period	First, last data	First, last data	First, last data	First, last period	First, last period
CTRL - ← CTRL - →	First, last data	First, last data	First, last data	First, last period	First, last period	First, last period	First, last data	First, last data
PGUP PGDN	Prior, next year	Prior, next year	Prior, next year	First, last data	First, last data	First, last data	Prior, next year	Prior, next year
CTRL - PGUP CTRL - PGDN	Change view	Change view	Change view	Change view	Change view	Change view	Change view	Change view
P S			Print, save view	Print, save view	Print, save view	Print, save view	Print, save view	Print, save view
ESC	Quit	Quit	Quit	Quit	Quit	Quit	Quit	Quit

The amount of memory in your PC may affect ValueWar's analyses. For example, if the PC has little memory, ValueWar may be unable to run strategy or scenario tests.

---

* Cannot perform this function in the indicated view, so ValueWar automatically changes to a view in which the function can be performed.

Keyboard Reference

	View-switch keys
Key	
SHIFT-F1	Value view
SHIFT-F2	Graph view
SHIFT-F3	Data-history view
SHIFT-F4	Financial-snapshot view
SHIFT-F5	Profit-and-loss view
SHIFT-F6	Competition view
SHIFT-F7	Scenario-test view (if scenario test run)
SHIFT-F8	Strategy-test view (if strategy test run)
CTRL-PGUP CTRL-PGDN or + & -	Prior/next view in loop

	Keyboard reference for other features			
Key	**Scenario menu**	**Strategy menu**	**Non-strat moves**	**Report**
F1	Help system	Help system	Help system	Help system
F2	Define scenario	Define strategy		Define scenario
F3				
F4				
F5				
F6				
F7				
F8				
F9				
F10				
↑↓	Point	Point	Specific NSMs	Scroll up and down
←→			Specific NSMs	
HOME END	First, last scenario	First, last strategy	Specific NSMs	Top, bottom
PGUP PGDN	Prior, next year	Prior, next year	Specific NSMs	Page up or down
INS			Use strategy	
ENTER	Select scenario	Select strategy	Select NSM	
P S				Print, save report
ESC	Back up (cancel)	Back up (cancel)	Back up (cancel)	Done with report

ndex

The page symbol	Indicates the section
A	*About ValueWar*
T	*ValueWar Tutorial*
R	*ValueWar Reference*

Index